The Perfect Guitar

To Michael

With appreciation
for our many
years of friendship

Rich

Published by Cadence House Press
142 Beechwood Avenue, Victoria, BC, Canada V8S 3W5

LIBRARY AND ARCHIVES CANADA CATALOGUING IN PUBLICATION

Gibbs, Richard
The Perfect Guitar: A Journey of Discovery/Richard Gibbs
ISBN 978-0-9948613-0-6

Printed in Canada

The Perfect Guitar

A Journey of Discovery in a Guitar Maker's Workshop

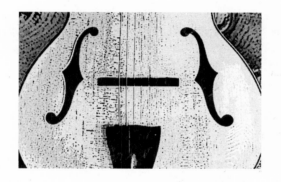

Rick Gibbs

CADENCE HOUSE PRESS

Victoria

For Pat, Matt and Claire

CONTENTS

Author's Note

1   Doubts and Dreams. 1

2   First Guitars 10

3   Seawater Sitka 18

4   Visionaries and Gardeners 29

5   Twisting Currents 37

6   Chisels, Planes and Spokeshaves. 44

7   Manzer and Metheny 50

8   Vows of Poverty, Visions of Success 63

9   Passion 70

10 Feel and Touch. 79

11 The Factory Versus The Workshop 87

12 D'Aquisto and D'Angelico. 96

13 Intoxication 102

14 The Middle Way 108

15 Big Trees 116

16 Eigenfrequencies 123

17   Art That Sings 131

18   Julian Lage 144

19   Frank Vignola/Bucky Pizzarelli 153

20   Go-Bars. 162

21   The Body Whole. . . .. .169

22   The Neck: Part One 175

23   The Neck: Part Two 187

24   French Polishing. 193

25   The Exploding Guitar. 204

26   A Kind of Perfection 214

Acknowledgements

Bibliography

Permissions

Ten Great Archtop Recordings

Websites

About the Author

Photos within the text by Robert Anderson and Rick Gibbs

AUTHOR'S NOTE

I've had a fifty-year love affair with the guitar. We've sometimes drifted apart, but I've always returned to that special feeling that comes when I sit on a couch and hold a guitar in my arms. Guitarists around the world will know what I'm talking about.

In 2010 my love turned into a quest when I wrote a magazine piece about luthiers, those highly skilled artisans who craft gorgeous stringed instruments in the quiet of their wood-scented workshops.

Later that year my quest expanded when I interviewed Linda Manzer, one of the great luthiers in the world and Pat Metheny, one of the great guitarists, for a CBC radio documentary called *Kindred Spirits: Linda Manzer's Thirty-Year Journey with Pat Metheny* that I wrote, produced and presented.

In 2012 my quest became an obsession when I commissioned Robert Anderson, an internationally recognized Victoria luthier, to build me an acoustic archtop guitar.

This book is about the remarkable journey of discovery that ensued.

"There may be a few in mind I remember as fine instruments but never the perfect one. That's what makes you go on to the next."

James D'Aquisto

The Perfect Guitar

One

DOUBTS AND DREAMS

I watched as luthier Robert Anderson placed the sixty-year-old guitar on the large wire-coiled sketchbook he'd laid on the bench in the centre of his workshop. An overhead light reflected off the guitar's mahogany surface, creating faint shadows on the white paper beneath. Daylight streaming through a window provided additional illumination as he perched his wire-rimmed reading glasses on his nose, picked up a flat carpenter's pencil and hunched his tall, long-limbed body over the guitar, centering it carefully on the page before placing the flat side of the pencil against the body near the neck.

"Put your hand on top and hold it steady for me."

"Here?" I said, reaching over and placing my hand on the strings near the twelfth fret, close enough to the body to hold the guitar still without getting in his way.

"That's good."

With his large hand Robert steadily traced the shape onto the paper by following the smaller curve of the upper bout, then the narrowed waist and finally the larger curve of the lower bout, before coming around

1

the bottom and reversing the sequence up the other side. The pencil scratched along the thick paper as I held the guitar still, hardly breathing for fear that I might accidentally move it.

Robert was designing and building an acoustic archtop guitar for me. As he worked, I planned to document the project while learning as much as I could about the history and craft of this unique instrument. I'd dreamed up the idea after revisiting two literary non-fiction books I'd read some years ago: Witold Rybczynski's *The Most Beautiful House in the World* and Tracy Kidder's *House*. Both tell the story of the building of a home, one in the countryside outside Montreal, where Rybczinski, an architect and writer teaching at McGill University, designed a house for himself and his wife after setting out to build a boat shed; the other in rural New England, where Kidder, a literary journalist, documented the building of a first home for a young couple near Amherst, Massachusetts. I'd returned to the books several times, fascinated by their blend of art, craft and philosophy.

Late one December night a few days before Christmas, I thought about writing a similar book about the designing and building of a guitar, an instrument I'd loved and played since my teens. What better way than to have my friend Robert build me the guitar of my dreams in the process? That night I emailed him my idea, adding the caveat, "It may be totally nuts and it may not work for any number of reasons but it has caught my fancy." Less than twenty-four hours later, he emailed back, "Let's do it!"

He was as crazy as I was obsessed.

A month later here we were, making a start. As Robert worked, my thoughts wandered to the tracing I did as a kid in the fifties and early sixties, sitting at our chrome-legged arborite kitchen table or lying on our beige wall-to-wall living room carpet with various objects – a cut-out picture, a leaf, my hand – and tracing their outlines onto sheets of paper I'd laid atop magazines. Sometimes I'd place tracing paper over cartoon figures in comic books and follow their lines with a soft-leaded pencil.

Years later as a student experiencing my first university drawing class, I'd sat at a group table creating 'contour drawings', where we traced objects – a paper bag, an old boot, a live model – by following their contours in space with our eyes while our pencil scraped blindly on a page in our sketchbooks in one continuous line. The process yielded wobbly lines that wandered dangerously off course and proportions out-of-whack. But the goal wasn't to create a finished sketch – the exercise was designed to free our hands and open our eyes, teaching the importance of letting go, of seeing, of visualizing.

It occurred to me that Robert was doing a kind of visualizing himself as he traced the outline of the guitar I'd provided as a model. He was an experienced guitar maker but this was his first archtop. I could sense him feeling his way with the project and with me. He was used to working on his own. Now he had me peering over his shoulder, watching every move.

We were both feeling our way, wondering how our project would turn out and what kind of experience it would be. I didn't know about Robert but I was concerned about how it might affect our friendship should things go awry. We'd be sitting here together nearly every week for a year. What if we had trouble getting along? What if the guitar he built wasn't what I'd hoped for?

I'd met Robert a few years before while on assignment for *Boulevard*, a local magazine that had contracted me to write a story on Vancouver Island luthiers. I'd pitched the idea after learning that some of the best guitar builders in Canada lived on the west coast and many were right here on the Island. I knew that Jean Larrivée, probably Canada's best known acoustic guitar builder, had set up his factory here in the late seventies, relocating it from Toronto to be closer to the west coast wood supply. He eventually moved the operation to Vancouver and then opened a second factory in California as he expanded his business worldwide. But Larrivée was producing factory-made guitars; I was on the hunt for artisans who built them by hand – one at a time.

I'd found Robert's name through an Internet search. I emailed him and he invited me to his workshop in 'Vic

West', an old neighbourhood across the harbour from downtown Victoria that had its heyday in the eighteen eighties and nineties, when many prominent Victoria families, including coal baron Robert Dunsmuir, had built homes there. Many of these houses with their hipped and gabled roofs, towers, widows-walks, and ornamented open porches survived, along with more modest working class homes in various stages of restoration and repair.

On a summer's day I found Robert's workshop situated at the end of a short street off Craigflower Road. With its gabled roof, wooden siding and wooden sash windows, his one-and-a-half-storey workshop fit right into the neighbourhood. It faced his home, a nineteenth-century farmhouse complete with hexagonal tower and wrap-around balustraded porch. In between was an inviting yard with a picket fence, winding path, grassy areas, small vegetable garden, dwarf apple trees and, in the curved beds that bordered the property, tangles of flowers, shrubs and trees that recalled informal Victorian cottage gardens of the past. I immediately felt at home and thought this was the place the magazine photographer should come to shoot photos to accompany the story. It was where a luthier should work because it spoke of a time when craftsmanship mattered and the wooden objects of our lives – tables, chairs, wardrobes, and, yes, guitars – were built slowly and built to last.

Inside the workshop, a warm, wooden-floored space

filled with the tools and objects of his trade – planes and spokeshaves, handsaws and chisels, a bandsaw and joiner, a router and drill press, moulds and jigs, stacks of wood and instruments-in-progress – I learned that Robert had begun his professional life as a draughtsman, had eventually become a self-employed architectural designer and project manager, and then had done what many dream of but never dare do – left behind a secure career to pursue his guitar-building passion. I was taken by the boldness of that move and the romance of his craft. I decided then and there that he would feature prominently in the magazine piece.

And he had a good story to tell. When he was only four he rode a train from Vancouver to Yorkton, Saskatchewan, to visit relatives. While playing in the attic of his uncle's farmhouse he spotted a guitar, "probably an old Gibson," he said. He remembered picking it up, setting the big instrument in his small lap and strumming it for so long he ended up with a blister on his thumb. That anecdote made it into the magazine piece and in fact began the story when I wrote, "Robert Anderson remembers exactly when his love affair with the guitar began." It was a story that showed just how hooked people could get on guitars.

The guitar Robert was tracing was a 1948 Harmony Patrician acoustic archtop I'd purchased several months before in a local guitar store. Harmony was the American company that supplied Sears with Silvertone guitars, the bright red electrics and the honey-coloured acoustics that graced the catalogues that people of my generation leafed through as kids. (How quaint that seems in the Internet age.) This particular model, an H1414, was apparently one of the company's better instruments. It was lightweight, a desirable characteristic in an acoustic guitar, and was made of solid wood as opposed to the cheaper plywoods often used. The wood was mostly mahogany with the exception of a broad strip of spruce that ran down the middle of the top and the rosewood fingerboard that graced the neck. Attractive but colour-mismatched block-design marquetry bound the body, and the headstock sported an elaborate vine inlay.

It was that inlay that first caught my eye. I'd been looking for such a guitar for a long time but was reluctant to spend the thousands needed to buy a vintage Gibson or Epiphone. One day the Harmony appeared like magic. The price was right and so I snapped it up. I liked the looks and it played well enough with good volume and projection, a hallmark of the archtop design because such guitars were originally intended to cut through a big band before amplifiers were common and electric guitars took over.

But I soon discovered a problem. Mildew was growing inside, likely the product of the guitar sitting for years in some damp basement or garage. I'd tried to remove it by spraying a bleach solution inside the body, but I couldn't get rid of the mildewy smell which wafted up every time I played. I'd decided that once Robert was

7

finished with it, the guitar would go up for resale.

I wanted an instrument I could pick up, wrap my arms around and play for hours at a time, never tiring of the sound, scent, feel or look. I wanted a guitar that would inspire me whenever I played it. I wanted a perfect guitar.

The tracing complete, Robert lifted the Harmony off the page and put it aside. He held the sketchbook under the light at arm's length as we pondered the shape. It looked acceptable but a doubt clouded my mind. Should we really be using this cheaper, mass-produced instrument as the model for an expensive handcrafted one-of-a-kind guitar? Robert shrugged off my concern.

"I don't think it's a problem. We're just using it to suggest and inspire our guitar. Tonight I'll take this tracing and reshape the body and adjust some of the dimensions."

"How will you do that?"

"I have some drafting tools that will help me redraw the curves but I'll do it mostly by intuition. I'll work the lines until I get something that feels right. I think we'll keep the sixteen-inch lower bout, but I'll probably flatten the bottom out a little to make it more pear-shaped."

Pear-shaped? I tried but couldn't get the image into my head. Perhaps sensing my hesitation, Robert said, "Tomorrow you can look at the drawing and see if you like it. You can approve the design I come up with."

I stepped from the warmth of the workshop into the cool January air, wondering what our next session would bring. As I got into my older silver-grey Honda Civic, I was hopeful and excited but also worried. Doubts drifted in as I drove down the road – the same concerns I'd had earlier about friendship and expectations.

Another more personal concern also intruded. In 1999 when I was teaching high school, a routine medical check-up revealed a chronic blood cancer that could become acute and threaten my life. The progress of the illness had already forced me to leave my teaching job and limit my activity. That, coupled with a family history that had seen my father killed in an accident at work when I was four, my mother felled by multiple myeloma thirteen years later when I was seventeen, and my only sibling, my older brother, taken by advanced melanoma when I was twenty-five (he was thirty-eight), had made me much more aware of my mortality. In the last few years, I had, with one exception, taken on only short writing projects – magazine articles mostly – because I knew I could see those through in the course of a month or two. This was a much bigger project with a much longer timeline. I wondered if I would finish the book or even see the guitar completed. Would I actually fulfill what could be my last creative dream?

Two

FIRST GUITARS

A September day in 1965. It's a Saturday morning and a fifteen-year-old kid in Keds, Levis, madras shirt and a light blue, hooded nylon K-Way is riding a cream coloured trolley bus down Commercial Drive in East Vancouver. The dark green vinyl seat under him feels hard as the bus whines, whirs and lurches its way towards the blue North Shore mountains, its trolley arms sparking and nearly jumping off the overhead wires every time it creeps through a busy intersection.

A particularly hard lurch jerks the kid to and fro in his seat, slightly dislodging his black horn-rimmed glasses that are taped on one temple with white adhesive tape. He adjusts them with one hand and lifts the small red transistor radio he holds in the other hand back to his ear where he once again hears the steady strum of the acoustic guitar and the edgy, nasally voice spilling out lyrics that are changing the world for him and a million other North American teenagers.

The bus turns left onto East Hastings and the kid looks up to get his bearings. He doesn't want to miss his stop. His destination is a pawnshop eight or ten blocks down the road. He's been there before but this is a special trip. Today he has money in his pocket.

I don't remember all the details of that bus ride, but the clothes, the glasses, the feel of those old Vancouver trolley buses, the route and the destination are right. I might have had my little transistor radio with me and Dylan's "The Times They Are A Changin'" could well have been playing on CFUN or CKLG, the AM stations I and every other kid in Vancouver would listen to while Red Robinson and Fred Latremouille spun the 45s we so craved.

Music was everything.

That ride took me right into the heart of Vancouver's notorious Downtown Eastside where the pawnshops were located. In those days it was perfectly safe for a young kid to roam the streets during the day because drug use was mostly hidden behind closed doors and venerable institutions like Woodward's Department Store and the Vancouver Museum flourished. I would often go downtown by myself on a Saturday morning, get off at Main and Hastings and wander around, day-dreaming and window-shopping my way west towards the downtown core at Georgia and Granville and on to Stanley Park.

On that particular day I must have walked into the pawnshop, taken some time to make a final decision, and then pulled the cash out of my wallet. The item

I bought was inside a black case lined with plush red fabric. I don't remember the brand name. I do remember the price – fifteen dollars.

I would have walked out of the store and carried the case to the bus stop for the return trip, holding it between my legs as I rode the trolley back home. At Victoria Drive and East 41st Avenue I would have gotten off the bus, squeezing through the rear folding doors and walking the five or so blocks to my house on East 42nd. Entering my room, I would have laid the case on my bed and opened it up, scarcely able to breathe.

I had purchased my first guitar.

First guitars are exciting but they can be cruel. When you are at your most vulnerable, when you know nothing, when the tips of your fingers are lily-tender, when you have the fine motor skills of a chimpanzee wielding a two-by-four, you're forced to push down hard on thin steel strings that refuse to yield. They cut into your fingertips, creating pain, unholy buzzes and rattles, and maybe, just maybe, the odd note that actually rings out for more than a second, giving you the faint hope that one day you'll actually be able to play that C, G and dreaded F chord in sequence and in time.

When Robert was thirteen and living in Nanaimo, his parents, knowing that he loved music, bought him his first guitar. "It was horrible. One of those Sears specials with super-high action, all uneven, and Black Diamond high tension strings. It's amazing I learned to play," he told me one day over lunch as he laughed and described the pain he went through fingering his first tentative notes and chords.

It's often said that the guitar is an easy instrument to play but it's not. You can pick up a few simple chords quickly, but it takes a long time to develop the dexterity to play them effectively and to make the transitions smooth. I remember spending hours learning to play a basic four-note F chord. Willing the fingers to depress those strings simultaneously without them buzzing took hundreds of repetitions. And that was just the beginning. There was still the problem of shifting from C to F and F to G. The latter was easier because you could open your hand and just grab the high E string at the third fret with your ring or baby finger. That gave you the four-note chord with just one string depressed. You could then add the two other fingers at your leisure on strings five and six to get the full sound with the bass included.

The C to F transition was much harder. You had to shift your index finger from holding down one string on the first fret to depressing two in the same position with a short "barre." Then you squeezed your middle finger onto the second fret and your ring finger onto the third. These motions had to happen simultaneously. In the end all the fingers were crammed together on a tiny patch of fretboard that seemed impossible to occupy. Getting the full C-F-G progression to be in time, smooth and musical took forever. Contrast that with a piano where anybody can bang out "Chopsticks" or a simple three-chord blues progression within five minutes of learning. Many people give up on the guitar because it's too hard to play.

I persisted, eventually mastering C, C7, F, G and adding D, D7 E, E7, Am, Dm, Dm7 and A – pretty well everything needed to play hundreds of popular songs. One of the first full songs I learned was "Kansas City," a Jerry Leiber and Mike Stoller rhythm-and-blues tune recorded by the Beatles early in their career. Once the chords were under my fingers, it was pretty easy to play and sing even for someone like me who didn't have a voice. I loved making the shift from the C to C7 by dropping my baby finger onto the G string at the third fret before shifting into that F chord. The colour created by that dominant seventh chord sounded so much better than the plain vanilla C, F, and G triads used in a zillion other songs.

Later I picked up various licks – the dum dum, dum de dum de dum dum of "Satisfaction" followed by the more complicated dum, de dah dah de dum, de dum de dah dah of "Daytripper". Other songs soon came along: The Beatles' "This Boy", "I Am A Rock" by Paul Simon and folk songs like "Michael Row the Boat Ashore."

Eventually I got rid of that fingertip-killer and in 1968 bought a beautiful one-hundred-dollar Yamaki dreadnought, a well-made Japanese guitar with low action that was a delight to play and that I could actually keep tuned. I was hooked, and, like millions of other kids strumming guitars throughout North America, I went on to learn Dylan, Donovan and Cohen, playing their songs through high school and into university while making feeble attempts at singing.

Robert, a few years younger than me, was on a similar journey, although he would go much further, following a path that would see him performing in public. He took lessons from a Nanaimo neighbour who played a Gretsch hollow-body electric guitar and whistled country tunes. The first song the neighbour taught him was Hank Williams' "Jambalaya" ("On the Bayou.") Robert would babysit the neighbour's kids in exchange for guitar lessons, quietly playing the Gretsch while the kids slept. Soon his parents got him his own electric guitar and he started learning Beatles' tunes and other songs of the day. Eventually he joined a band.

In the summer of 1969 after finishing grade eleven, he bought a backpack, slung his Sears acoustic guitar over his shoulder and hitchhiked with a couple of friends to the Okanagan Valley in the British Columbia interior to pick fruit.

He'd been working for a few weeks and enjoying his new-found freedom when another picker suggested they go right across Canada. He jumped at the chance, taking his guitar with him and playing every opportunity he could, busking on the streets of Winnipeg and Toronto and even getting thrown out of a Yorkville folk club because he was under age. A picture from the time shows a tall, shirtless, skinny-armed kid, sporting thick red hair, a budding moustache and Neil Young sideburns, sitting in a folding lawn chair on his uncle's porch in Toronto looking into the camera as he plays his guitar with its bent tuning peg in the summer heat.

When he returned to Victoria for his last year of high school – his parents had moved back to Victoria where he was born – he started learning Dylan, Cohen and Donovan songs and took his guitar to school. In good weather he'd sit outside playing and singing and other students would join in.

He turned away from the electric guitar. "I became much more interested in the acoustic guitar at that point because of how it fed me – how it helped build my social life and helped me make friends."

Songs of romance and protest, like "Suzanne," "Catch the Wind," and "The Times They Are A Changin'" were also feeding him. He could relate much better to their melodies, harmonies and lyrics than to the rock music of the day, which he saw as overly aggressive. "Rock was for tough guys. I wasn't a tough guy."

Victoria had a rock scene and he had friends who were involved but he wasn't interested. "Having hitchhiked across the country and slept in shelters and ridden the railways and having met lots of different kinds of people, I was aware that there were certain kinds of people who revelled in sinking down, in getting drunk too much, in doing hard drugs, in abusing themselves, and I didn't want to be like that." To him the rock scene was too seedy, too close to the toothless down-and-outers he'd encountered on the road, and so he chose a different path by performing at folk venues around town – coffee houses hosted by the YMCA, the Boys Club, and the University of Victoria.

Stage fright affected him, but he was inspired by musical heroes like The Beatles and got through it. "I wanted to be like them, I wanted to be like those people up on the stage, playing and singing and having a great time." As he grew more comfortable, he realized that performing fulfilled him. "I didn't get that anywhere else in my life – that sense of something bigger than me – the audience was there – it wasn't just me playing in my room."

Three

SEAWATER SITKA

The day after we traced the Harmony I returned to Robert's workshop to see how he'd made out with the design. I arrived under a blue January sky to find that he'd redrawn the body shape, broadening the lower bout and reducing the upper to create a less extreme curve at the waist. It looked good. He'd also sketched in f-holes, the violin-like sound holes that would be cut into the top. We'd agreed to go that route rather than using the round sound hole typically used in flat-top guitar construction. A round or oval hole was said to create more warmth and was occasionally used in archtop guitars, but I preferred the look of traditional f-holes, providing we could get a good bass sound. Robert said if we kept the guitar as light as possible, a quality he always strived for in his instruments, the bass, mid-range and treble tones should all be good because the lighter the instrument, the more responsive it would be to the vibrations of the strings.

With the body shape decided, we turned to the chunk of wood standing at the far end of Robert's bench that he'd showed me the previous day after doing the tracing. "Looks like a piece of firewood, doesn't it?" he'd joked then.

Indeed with its splinters, greyed ends, and rough-hewn surface, the block destined to become the top of my guitar had looked like it was ready for an axe and would burn nicely in a fireplace, crackling and sparking as it turned to embers and ash. As he'd laid it on the bench to check its length, width and thickness, I'd recalled that it had a special provenance. It was a piece of Sitka spruce from Vancouver Island that had been underwater for fifty years or more.

Robert had told me the story when I interviewed him for the piece I'd written for *Boulevard*. Some years ago, when he was still working in construction as a project manager and building guitars part time, his friend Jim Ham, a double bass builder in Victoria, contracted him to build a new workshop under his carport. Before the work could start, a stack of cut-up dock pilings that had been air drying for over twenty years had to be moved. (Luthiers consider air-dried, as opposed to kiln-dried, the best wood for instrument making.) Ham had planned to use the wood to make double basses but it was now in the way. He offered some of it to Robert, who cut and split it into guitar-sized chunks before moving it to his own workshop.

Robert believed that the mineralization that had occurred from submersion in the ocean gave it special qualities that contributed to its value in making guitar tops. He explained that Antonio Stradivari and other

Cremonese builders had likely used wood submerged in the salt water lagoons of Venice to create their violins. While no one could prove it, it was thought by some that the mineralization was partly responsible for the quality of their sound. Robert had been using his supply for a number of years and felt it made his instruments unique.

If it didn't affect the sound, it did give them a unique appearance. His 'Seawater Sitka,' as he called it, had a warmer, darker hue than conventional Sitka spruce.

Whatever its origin, when I looked at the chunk of 'firewood' for the first time, I could hardly believe it would become the finely carved top of my first hand-built guitar.

It looked less rough now. Robert had scraped and planed the faces to remove the splinters and ridges before I'd arrived that morning and was preparing to saw one edge to get a flat surface. As he started his bandsaw and began cutting, the blade bound slightly, producing little wisps of smoke that left an acrid smell hanging in the air. But he got a satisfactory cut and the chunk now had a flat edge he could lay on the bandsaw table that would allow him to slice it in half lengthwise. Before doing this crucial operation, he decided he should change the blade and make some adjustments.

While he prepared the saw, I sat at his desk making notes and reflecting on how good it felt to be in this warm, light-filled space with wood and tools all around.

Through the window in front of the desk I could see the tops of the big evergreens that edged his property swaying in a stiff breeze that had arrived with a weather change. A large patch of sunlight stretched across the lawn and garden, the shadows of the trees dancing within it. All was quiet except for the gentle whir of the heat pump warming his shop and Robert's metallic tinkering as he fitted the new blade. I could sense the satisfaction he got working here. He had me to contend with now, but most of the time he was on his own and could absorb himself completely in his craft.

I thought about efficiency as Robert worked at the bandsaw, realizing that for each procedure, he had to reset his tools. Linda Manzer, a Toronto luthier who has built guitars for the likes of Pat Metheny, Liona Boyd and Bruce Cockburn, had told me that she got tired of adjusting her lone router, a common power tool frequently used in guitar construction. Her solution was to buy multiple routers and set each one differently so she could quickly grab the one needed for a particular job.

In a guitar factory the jobs are compartmentalized, one builder prepares the tops, another the backs, a third the sides. Here Robert did every operation himself, recalibrating his tools each time. For the re-sawing of the top he not only had to change and then adjust the blade but also make freehand test cuts on scrap pieces of wood to compensate for the tendency of bandsaw blades to skew to one side. The fitting and adjustments had already taken him nearly half an hour. I began to understand why hand-built guitars were more expensive than factory-built models. They were much more labour intensive. It remained to be seen the difference that would make in the quality of the instrument.

Robert was ready. The saw jolted into action and the blade, a long narrow loop of steel with fine teeth on one side, began running vertically around two enclosed wheels that drove it at a screaming three thousand feet per minute. Robert set the freshly-cut spine of the block of wood (the 'billet' he called it) on the bandsaw table and slowly pushed the leading edge into the blurred teeth, holding it steady and guiding it straight as he sawed it right down the middle to produce two almost identical 'bookmatched' halves, each about an inch-and-a-half thick.

He turned off the saw, laid the halves side-by-side on his workbench and contemplated them. "That wasn't a very good cut," he said, noting that the blade had twisted during the process. "I won't use that blade again." I felt a twinge of concern, thinking that the poor cut could affect the quality of the top. Maybe perfection wasn't going to be so easy to achieve after all.

Robert decided that with his joiner and bench-top thickness sander he could rescue the pieces and so he set to work squaring and smoothing them. I assisted him as we passed them through the sander with Robert on one side feeding them in and me on the other guiding them out. It felt good to be more than an observer, to feel the wood in my hands and to understand the patience required by a luthier. We stood there for probably twenty minutes, passing each piece through many times, slowly refining them.

Peering at our mirrored halves once again, Robert could read them like a book. He pointed to wider gaps between the grain lines that indicated the years when rainfall had been normal. Narrow gaps showed times of drought. Because the wood was from a relatively dry area of Vancouver Island, the widest gap was barely the thickness of a dime, whereas the lines nearly touched at the narrowest.

"How many lines per inch?" I asked, displaying some of the knowledge I'd picked up through research.

"Let's count them and see."

Robert laid a small metal ruler across one of the boards and began counting. He came up with an average of twenty.

A piece of Sitka spruce from one of the giants that grows in the rain-drenched Carmanah Valley on the west side of Vancouver Island or across the Strait of Juan de Fuca on the Olympic Peninsula – where up to twelve feet of rain can fall in a year – might have as few as four or five lines per inch because of rapid growth. Robert's wood was dense and tightly grained due to slow growth, a characteristic that, according to some sources, could improve its sound.

Open a piano top and you'll see a board under the

strings called the soundboard. Like a guitar top, its job is to amplify the vibrations produced when the strings are struck by the hammers. The sound board acts much like the paper cone or diaphragm of a speaker that vibrates in response to electrical signals transmitted through the speaker's coil.

In the case of pianos and guitars, European and North American spruce is generally considered to be the ideal tonewood, producing the clearest, most resonant, most sustained sound, while still being strong enough to stand up to use. The Steinway Piano Company uses Sitka spruce from British Columbia and Alaska with eight to twelve grain lines per inch. The company claims the more lines, the better the sound because the vibrations, they say, travel better in tighter-grained wood, just as cars move more efficiently on a multi-lane highway than on a single-lane road.

In 2004 Henri Grissino-Mayer, a tree-ring scientist at the University of Tennessee and Lloyd Burckle, a climatologist at Columbia University, added to the many theories about why violins built by Stradivari and his contemporaries sound so good. They suggested that these instruments, with their European spruce tops, would have been built with wood that grew very slowly during the Little Ice Age that occurred in Europe between 1400 and 1800. That slow growth would have created a tight grain, possibly enhancing the acoustical quality of the wood.

John Topham, a tree-ring expert and violin builder

in Surrey, England, quoted in *National Geographic's* online news, said the theory was interesting but not supported by his own observations. He noted that the Stradivarius violins he'd worked on over the years were built from wood with both narrow and wide spacing between the grain lines.

I asked Robert about it and he said that such issues are regularly debated in luthier forums. His take was that no one really knows for sure how important the character of the grain is since so many factors go into the building of a stringed instrument, making it difficult to isolate just one.

Robert Benedetto, one of the foremost builders of archtop guitars in the world today – his guitars sell for as much as $50,000 and are played by some of the best players in the world – would probably agree. He has long argued that the skill of the builder is by far the most important factor. To prove his point, he once built a guitar from knotty pine, a cheap wood riddled with small knots, checking and discolouration. He says it sounds as good as his instruments built from prime tonewoods. The debate continues.

Robert prepared the billet halves for gluing by running each through the joiner to produce smooth, square edges that would mate perfectly, held not by white carpenter's glue but by 'hide' glue. Prepared from hides, hooves, and other excess parts of cows and horses, hide glue is a colloidal substance much like gelatin that creates a molecular bond with itself. Found on the caskets of Egyptian pharaohs and in the woodwork of the Greeks and Romans, it was apparently used over thirty-thousand years ago by Palaeolithic cave artists in their paints to protect against moisture. Furniture makers and bookbinders used hide glue for centuries as did stringed instrument builders.

Robert used standard white carpenter's glue on his first few instruments but learned about hide glue from Jim Ham. Ham convinced him it was a better choice. Unlike modern glues that leave a film between the joined pieces, hide glue produces a wood-to-wood joint that isn't subject to 'creep' under pressure. The joint is stronger than the wood itself and is reversible with the application of heat and steam. It can be re-glued without removing the old material because hide glue sticks to itself even after being cured, unlike a modern glue that once cured will not adhere again. Luthiers repairing and restoring violins and guitars built with hide glue can completely disassemble them because of this property, making the repair and restoration work easier and better.

Aside from the technical benefits, it was clear from the way he handled the glue and talked about it that Robert valued the fact he was using a natural product unassociated with the petroleum industry. I watched as, ritual-like, he scooped a few spoonfuls of amber flakes and granules from a small jar and mixed them with some water he had heating in a little electric pot on his bench, explaining that the glue had to be hot to remain a liquid, with the ideal temperature being about 145 degrees Farenheit. It was both science and alchemy.

As he aligned the planks, I expected him to pull out several bar clamps of the sort I used in a high school woodworking class to clamp together individual boards to make a tabletop. I recalled spreading white glue on the edges of the boards, fitting them together and then spacing the clamps at regular intervals, tightening them gradually to increase the pressure and mate the pieces. With a damp cloth we then wiped away excess glue that had seeped out and left the whole assembly to set and cure. The next day we removed the clamps and then had a single board that could be planed smooth.

He surprised me with a much simpler system. He grabbed a roll of blue masking tape and began tearing off short strips, hinging the boards together like a book. He applied the tape with one plank flat on the bench and the other angled up at about forty-five degrees, explaining that when he lowered the angled plank, the tension in the tape would pull the boards tightly together. He then warmed the joint edges with a heat gun to give the hide glue a longer 'open time' before it set. I found it hard to believe that this technique would work but watched with anticipation as he finished applying the tape.

Checking the planks one last time and satisfied that they mated well, he dipped his brush into the glue pot, brushed the glue along both edges and then lowered the elevated board. Sure enough the two boards pulled tightly together. He examined the joint, thought he saw a slight gap, and decided to use one bar clamp as a precaution. That clamp in place, Robert declared the task done, and said he'd leave the boards to dry overnight before moving on to the next step.

Our chunk of 'firewood' was now ready to be carved into a guitar top.

Four

VISIONARIES AND GARDENERS

An archtop guitar is distinguished from a flat-top primarily by its arched top and back and its f-holes. Think big violin or small cello. It's the kind of guitar you'll see in its electric form around the neck of Scotty Moore in early pictures of him playing with Elvis Presley, or, going back to the big band era before electric guitars emerged, in its original acoustic form on the lap of Freddie Green who played rhythm guitar for the Count Basie Orchestra. Wes Montgomery played an amplified acoustic archtop as does UK solo jazz guitar master Martin Taylor. You'll even see a semi-hollow Gretsch electric archtop hanging from the neck of George Harrison in early photos of the Beatles.

Archtops are far less common than flat-tops and are favoured by jazz players for the sound they produce, which is typically more balanced between bass, mid-range and treble tones. It's a sound that lends itself to the fluid solo lines and rhythm accompaniment often heard in jazz. Country musicians and some rock players also favour electric hollow-body archtops, but the acoustic archtop – the type Robert was building for me – is most often associated with jazz.

Guitars are 'chordophones,' instruments that produce sound through one or more vibrating strings stretched between two points. Violins, banjos, mandolins and pianos are other examples.

The earliest-known chordophone is the musical bow which is depicted in prehistoric cave paintings in southern France and has been found in various cultures around the world. It looks like a hunting bow and was probably invented when ancient hunters were sitting around the campfire roasting meat and killing time. It's played to this day in Africa and Appalachia.

Sound is produced when the taut string is plucked, scraped or struck, causing vibrations to generate sound waves. One end of the bow can be placed in the player's mouth, which acts as a resonator, amplifying those waves and giving the player control over the character and dynamics of the sound. A dried gourd or other type of resonant chamber can be attached directly to the bow to increase the volume and add a different character.

From this starting point it's easy to imagine how the guitar evolved, like petroglyphs becoming Picassos. The bent stick became a carved neck, the resonating gourd a constructed sound box. A bridge was developed to raise the strings, a headstock and tuning pegs added to anchor them at the top and adjust the pitch. One string became six. Other refinements would follow – metal frets, pickguards, fine tonewoods, beautiful finishes.

As with all arts and crafts, the combination of leisure time, inventiveness, and the insatiable human desire to improve and refine our creations produced the vibrant universe of guitars we know today.

The lute and the oud, a Moorish instrument that emerged in Iberia in the eighth century, are often considered the immediate antecedents of the guitar, but stringed instruments have existed for thousands of years, making it difficult to trace the exact lineage.

Etymology echoes this situation. Our English word guitar comes from the Spanish *guitarra*, itself a derivative of the Greek *kithara* (Latin *cithara*). There's also the Arabic *qitara*, suggesting Middle Eastern roots and links to the instruments of India – it's probably no accident that 'guitar' sounds like 'sitar.'

The earliest guitars that emerged in Spain during the Renaissance were flat-top instruments with round sound holes. It wasn't until the turn of the twentieth century, when one builder in particular wondered why a mandolin or guitar couldn't be built like violins, violas, and cellos that a new approach would be tried and the archtop, with its carved top and back, would emerge a few hundred years after the flat-top.

Drive west along Interstate 94 from Detroit and in two hours you'll find yourself in Kalamazoo, Michigan, the birthplace of the modern archtop guitar. Today Kalamazoo is a town of 75,000, known largely for its craft breweries and medical supply companies. In the late nineteenth century, when Orville Gibson, a moustached young store clerk, first wandered its dirt-filled, board-walked streets, some twenty-thousand people lived in the area, many of them producing products the town was famous for – windmills, cast-iron stoves and horse-drawn buggies.

Gibson was born in Chateaugay, New York, in 1856 but moved to Kalamazoo sometime in the 1880s. He worked as a clerk, first in a shoe store and later in a restaurant, but his passion was designing and building stringed instruments from old pieces of furniture, wood that he valued for its durability and quality and was readily available. Working in his spare time, he built a number of sophisticated and complex mandolins that were innovative in structure and whimsical in design. They frequently featured black-painted surfaces and elaborate scroll-work and inlays – including an inlay that became his personal hallmark, an occult star-and-crescent, an appropriate insignia given the spiritualist age in which he lived.

In 1896 when he was forty, Gibson quit his day job and began building full time, opening a shop at 114 South Burdick and selling to local players. He'd joined the mandolin wave that hit the shores of America in the 1850s and surged across the country in the 1880s with the rapid increase in European immigration, including many Italian immigrants who brought with them exotic bowl-backed mandolins that became the rage, causing the Montgomery Ward catalogue of 1897 to remark on the "phenomenal growth in our Mandolin trade." The growth would continue well into the twentieth century with mandolin ensembles touring the vaudeville circuits, virtuoso players performing in concert halls, and mandolin orchestras and clubs forming in schools and colleges throughout the country but particularly in the South, often with the help and encouragement of the manufacturers.

Through experimentation Gibson learned to build better mandolins by using the principles of violin-building where the top and back of the instrument were carved from solid wood, rather than being formed by bending and assembling separate wood strips as was the case in the traditional bowl-back mandolin design. Believing that unstressed carved wood was significantly more sensitive than wood bent under tension, Gibson even cut the sides or rims from solid wooden blocks rather than bending them from thin strips. Through these methods he enhanced what he called "the sensitive resonance" and "vibratory action" of his instruments, producing a greater "power and quality of tone and melody." On May 11,1896 he filed for a patent to protect his design. On February 1, 1898, US Patent No. 598,245 was issued in his name.

Interested parties soon saw the commercial potential in Gibson's work. In 1900 a group of businessmen approached him, proposing the formation of a manufacturing company to produce instruments under his patent. In October 1902 they created a limited partnership, purchasing Gibson's patent rights and establishing the Gibson Mandolin-Guitar Manufacturing Company. Three of the partners were Kalamazoo lawyers and two were in the retail music business. Gibson was not a member of the partnership but received income from royalties and later from an annual consultant's fee. He was one of the company's first investors, buying sixty shares of company stock in November 1902.

Gibson maintained his association for about a decade during which time the company produced not only mandolins but also oval-holed archtop guitars, the immediate ancestor of the design we know today. Physical and possibly mental illness forced him to return to New York State in 1911 where he was hospitalized at least twice. He died of chronic endocarditis – inflammation of the inner lining of the heart – on his birthday in 1918, a few months before the end of the First World War. He was sixty-two.

If Orville Gibson was the visionary who broke the ground and planted the seeds that allowed the archtop to spring from the fertile soil of the Gibson Mandolin-Guitar Company, Lloyd Loar (1886-1943) was the master gardener who oversaw its growth and development. Loar joined the company in 1911 (the year Orville returned to New York) as a musician, composer and concert master charged with ensuring that the travelling groups demonstrating Gibson instruments would give compelling performances that would show off the tonal qualities of the instruments and entice audiences to buy them.

In 1919, following a six-month stint overseas as an entertainer with the American Expeditionary Force (AEF), Loar returned to Gibson, this time as an acoustical engineer and instrument designer. To these tasks he brought not only a sensitive musical ear but also a keen scientific mind. These attributes, combined with his exploratory spirit and singular focus, led to the development of several highly influential instruments at Gibson, most notably the F-5 mandolin and the L-5 archtop guitar.

Introduced in 1922, the L-5 is the standard by which all modern archtops are judged and the master template by which they are designed. It was the first archtop to feature f-holes, an adjustable floating bridge, a carved and graduated 'tap-tuned' top, an adjustable truss rod in the neck, parallel tone bars (braces), and a metal tailpiece. Beyond these attributes – or because of them – it was a powerful instrument able to cut through a big band without amplification and quickly became a key rhythm instrument in the dance bands and combos of the twenties, thirties and forties. Today a vintage L-5 in decent condition can fetch $50,000 or more.

Given the pivotal role dance-bands had in the development of the modern jazz guitar, first as a rhythm instrument and second (once it was electrified) as a solo instrument that could play convincing single-note lines, it can be argued that by developing the L-5, Loar transformed the guitar into a jazz instrument. Eddie Lang, considered by many the first jazz guitar virtuoso, played an L-5 as did Wes Montgomery, the player who would transform the sound of the instrument in the 1960s.

Scanning through the old Gibson ads collected in Adrian Ingram's book *The Gibson L-5*, one sees a who's who of jazz guitar giants, including Barney Kessel, Herb Ellis and Kenny Burrell. Other key players such as Freddie Green may not have played an L-5, but they played instruments modelled after it, providing further weight to the argument that by creating the L-5, Lloyd Loar created the modern jazz guitar.

The development of the violin in the early Renaissance made the development of the archtop in the twentieth century possible. Loar and Gibson both held the violin in high esteem, considering it to be one of the most acoustically efficient instruments ever produced. Inspired by Stradivari and his disciples, they transferred the principles of violin construction to the building of the archtop guitar, thus creating a new sound and a new instrument.

Five

TWISTING CURRENTS

Around the time I bought my second guitar, the Yamaki, I started to read Hermann Hesse, the Nobel-Prize-winning German writer whose literature of self-knowledge and enlightenment – *Journey to the East, Siddhartha, The Glass-Bead Game, Narcissus and Goldmund*, and *Steppenwolf* – inspired at least two generations of seekers, the first a German-speaking one in the twenties and the second the international counter-cultural youth movement of the sixties. I'd emerged from adolescence – for me a time of darkness and confusion – with a thirst for self-discovery. Glimmers of that quest appeared as early as age sixteen when I began writing poetry and reading about yoga, but it wasn't until my intellect was more developed and I'd escaped the emotional chaos of high school that I began to understand my nature – I was a seeker. The music I played, the books I read, and the activities I undertook were all part of a journey of self-discovery.

My mother died shortly after I turned seventeen. Because my father had been killed in a work accident when I was four and I was now on my own, I moved in with my brother and his family. It was the middle of grade twelve and it meant changing schools. They lived in Coquitlam, a Vancouver suburb behind Burnaby Mountain where Simon Fraser University is located. I could see a concrete structure atop the mountain whenever I walked to and from my new high school. I would sometimes pause and look up at it, thinking it was part of the campus, although I learned later it was actually a control tower of some sort. As I finished grade twelve and entered grade thirteen to take my first university-level courses, that tower became a symbol, a manifestation of my desire to better myself after a turbulent adolescence that had drained my confidence. I would get there. I would go to that university. That voice would keep speaking until I enrolled at SFU in the fall of 1968. I was eighteen.

When Robert was eighteen he was on a different path. Already married with a baby, he needed to find work. A year of unpleasant labouring jobs persuaded him to advance his education, but he didn't have the money for university, and so he turned to the employment programs offered by the Canadian government. Occupational testing revealed that his manual dexterity was off-the-scale, so high in fact that his employment counsellor told him he could be a brain surgeon.

He certainly had the intelligence. In high school, despite his best efforts to fit in with a group of rebellious long-haired types who smoked pot at lunch, he'd achieved A's, particularly in math, where he was moved into an advanced experimental class. Calculus and algebra – subjects that confounded me in high school – came easily to him.

Unfortunately, his financial and personal circumstances meant that becoming a brain surgeon – or pursuing any university degree for that matter – was out of the question, and so the counsellor, noting his manual abilities, suggested trying the one-year draughting program at Camosun College in Victoria. Robert enrolled, liked it, and a year later began working in the trade. He didn't know it then, but he'd taken a first step on a life journey that would lead him to the art and craft of guitar building.

Like all North American kids growing up in the fifties and sixties Robert and I experienced directly the increasing significance of the guitar in modern culture. It probably first penetrated my awareness when Elvis Presley appeared on the Ed Sullivan show in September 1956 with his Martin D-28 dreadnought slung over his neck. Named for a class of powerful, heavily-armoured WWI battleships, that large-bodied acoustic guitar, introduced by the Martin Guitar Company in 1931 and prized by musicians for its superior tone and projection, was already an iconic instrument played by the likes of country artist Hank Williams; but when sixty million people saw Elvis strumming, swaying and gyrating his way through "Hound Dog," his D-28 more theatrical prop than instrument, the guitar as cultural icon rocketed into the popular imagination.

Even before Elvis, Bill Haley lit up the airwaves in 1954 with the electric guitar sounds of "Rock Around the Clock." And before him Les Paul thrilled listeners with his revolutionary multi-tracked electric guitar work on "How High the Moon," a song he recorded with Mary Ford in 1951. I was only a kid, but I heard those songs on record and radio because my mother had a collection of 78s, and my brother, who was thirteen years older than me, collected 45s and LPs. He often had the radio on, tuned into Red Robinson, Vancouver's first rock-and-roll deejay. As well, because we had one of the first TVs on our block, I'd occasionally see musical performances on one of the few channels then available by roof-top antenna in Canada.

Early rock set the stage for a now-familiar timeline of rock and roll history – Buddy Holly and the Everly Brothers, The Ventures and the Beach Boys, the Beatles and the British Invasion. In the late 1950s and early 1960s our world was transformed by the guitar.

It wasn't just rock that brought this change. The folk revolution, with artists like Joan Baez, gave musical voice to the civil rights movement and spawned a singer-songwriter revolution led by the likes of Bob Dylan, Joni Mitchell, Gordon Lightfoot and Leonard Cohen. Other singer-songwriters like Paul Simon emerged not only as great lyricists but also as skilled guitarists who went well beyond mere strumming. (Joan Baez and Joni

Mitchell belong in this category as well – Baez for her fingerpicking technique that Dylan tried to learn but couldn't, and Mitchell for her unique open tunings that gave popular music vibrant new sounds and textures.)

Meanwhile electric guitar innovators like Jimi Hendrix, Jeff Beck, Carlos Santana, Eric Clapton and George Harrison were charging the air and the airwaves with their licks, rhythms and riffs and turning their guitars into powerful lead instruments with voices as unique and compelling as the vocals of a Van Morrison, a Janis Joplin or a Mick Jagger.

Older, already-established genres spoke too. The British blues invasion led by groups like the Rolling Stones, The Animals, and Cream sparked a blues and roots renaissance that opened white kids' ears on both sides of the Atlantic, mine included, to black artists like B.B. King, Muddy Waters and Sonny Terry and Brownie McGee – and their guitars.

New international guitar sounds joined the flood when jazz guitarist Charlie Byrd collaborated with saxophonist Stan Getz on *Desifinado*, a 1962 album that introduced northern ears to the rhythms of bossa nova and to South American artists like Antonio Carlos Jobim and Joao Gilberto.

Mainstream jazz was there, too, most notably in the work of Wes Montgomery whose innovative technique (he used his thumb, not a pick) and approach (polyphonic solos created from melodic single-note lines, parallel octave lines, and block chords) changed the sound of the guitar forever and inspired many of the great players of our time.

All these musical tributaries combined into a vast river of song that swept an entire generation along in its twisting, turning currents. At the heart of it all was the guitar, an instrument that became synonymous with the flood of musical and cultural change.

Growing up in that milieu I couldn't help but develop a love for the guitar and the tones it could project from the poetic to the perverse. The guitar could be warm and lyrical or rebellious, loud and dirty – and everything in between. More than any other instrument it adopted the character and mood of the player. Fingers on strings meant a direct connection to the instrument, with no mechanical device – be it piano key and hammer or saxophone mouthpiece and reed – to get in the way. Jerry Lee Lewis might climb atop his piano stool and bang away on the keys but Jimi Hendrix could lay his guitar on the stage between his legs and literally light it on fire. The guitar was immediate, tactile and charged with energy – you could hold it your arms and feel it in a way that was impossible with any other instrument. It was also democratic – guitars didn't cost a lot; almost anyone could own one.

The piano, the instrument of choice for earlier generations, was more staid. It lived in the parlour or, in a later era, the living room where people could gather around and be led in song. The guitar was so portable it could easily shift from the public to the personal, and more often than not served as an instrument of reflection and introspection in the hands of teenagers seeking knowledge, freedom and quietude in their own bedrooms.

One of Brian Wilson's most evocative songs, "In My Room," co-written with Gary Usher, speaks of a place free of fear and worry, a refuge where secrets can be told, the past released and the future imagined. Hundreds of thousands of young people of my generation found refuge in their rooms and dreamed their futures with their arms wrapped around a guitar, quietly strumming the chords and learning the melodies of the music that was changing their lives.

The sixties and early seventies also sparked a renaissance in instrument-making. Folk musicians were playing not only guitars but also simpler stringed instruments like dulcimers. In an era of alternative lifestyles and widespread interest in the creation of self-made handcrafted objects, aspiring players sometimes built their own instruments from kits or from scratch. They might build a dulcimer first but then graduate to an acoustic guitar. From these early experiments on kitchen tables and bedroom desks, modern lutherie was born as the guitar became the most popular instrument on earth.

Six

CHISELS, PLANES AND SPOKESHAVES

When I arrived for our third session, I discovered that Robert was ready to cut out the guitar top and begin carving. He'd already used the modified tracing from our first session to construct a mould that would be used in this process.

Unlike the mould a child might use to turn a blob of plasticine into a figurine, Robert's mould wasn't designed to shape a malleable material. Rather it would act first as a template and then as a form in which the body of the guitar could be built.

Robert had constructed it by gluing pieces of plywood together into a rectangular 'sandwich' about two inches thick, twenty inches wide and two feet long. He'd then laid the drawing of the body on the sandwich and used a small tool to scribe the shape through the paper onto the surface. He'd then cut it out, leaving behind a guitar-shaped hole. He'd then cut around the perimeter, leaving a mould that was a few inches wide with a rectangular tab protruding at each end. He'd drilled a small hole sideways through each tab and then cut the mould in half lengthwise. He'd reconnected the halves with bolts and wing nuts installed in the tabs, allowing them to work together as a single entity or to be separated as needed during various stages of the guitar-building process.

Today it would be a template. Robert centered the mould atop our glued plank and with a pencil traced

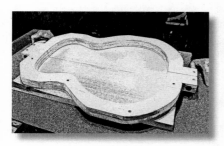

the guitar shape onto the surface. He then took the plank over to his bandsaw and carefully cut it out, leaving an eighth-inch border all around the traced line. We now had a Sitka spruce plank that was the basic shape of the guitar top.

Robert was familiar with everything he'd done to this point. Now it was time to venture into new and potentially treacherous terrain as he transformed this inch-thick guitar-shaped plank into a light, resonant soundboard that would become the top of my guitar.

I wondered how this would go as I contemplated the task ahead. Everything up to now had been done mostly by machine and measurement. These were operations I understood. I couldn't see how Robert was going to remove as much as eighty percent of the material by hand and end up with an arched, graduated top that was flexible, resonant and symmetrical. How would he know how deep to carve and how much material to remove at a time? How would he keep the arch symmetrical and know when to stop carving? I recognized that it would take days to complete the process and that the further along he got, the more likely it was that he could make a mistake that would mean starting all over again.

It was time to begin. He clamped the guitar top to his bench and began planing around the perimeter with a small German-made 'gents plane,' so-called because in earlier times this type of plane was used by gentlemen who did woodworking as a hobby and had no need for the full-sized, heavy-duty tools used by everyday carpenters. Made of European red beech with a horn-beam sole, it was much lighter than a metal plane. Robert said he liked it because it was less tiring, but when he handed it to me, I felt the warmth of wood instead of the cold of metal in my hand, and I sensed that the attraction went beyond energy conservation. Light, warm and smooth, it felt like an extension of my own body. I imagined it connected the woodworker more closely to his work, as well as to the long line of traditional craftsmen who had used such a tool.

There was also something about using wood on wood. Except for the blade, in its very construction a gents plane was closer to nature than an all-steel implement forged in fire and machined with taps and dies and grinders and drills. I was beginning to understand that while Robert used power tools to save time, he loved simpler, more natural processes and techniques.

He worked with short quick strokes, gradually piling up curled shavings that were soon spilling off the edge of the bench and onto the floor. His initial goal was to thin the top around the perimeter, starting about two-and-a-half inches in and angling the edge down towards the surface of his workbench. The soundboard would be thinnest at its outer edge, thickening towards the middle. This graduated shape would allow it to vibrate like the skin of a drum while remaining strong enough to resist the stress of the strings.

Because he had a lot of material to remove, he soon turned to a wooden-handled chisel and a carver's mallet to speed up the process. Looking remarkably like a WWII German 'potato masher' hand grenade, the mallet was made of lignum vitae (wood of life), a type of ironwood so  dense that it would sink in water. More than twice as hard as hickory, it was the hardest trade wood in the world. Traditionally it had been used to make everything from croquet mallets to belaying pins on old sailing ships.

I held the mallet and it felt remarkably balanced. Robert explained that unlike a hammer, it wouldn't damage the wooden handles of his chisels. He was soon banging off shavings a sixteenth of an inch thick that were piling up so quickly that he said with regret, "I'm turning what could be three great flat-top guitar tops into shavings!"

I asked him what else he was thinking as he worked. He said he was finding the process fascinating. Using hand tools he was learning more about the qualities of the Sitka spruce he'd used for years to build his flat-top guitars. For one thing it was much harder than he'd expected. With his flat-tops he'd always used machines to saw and sand the tops to a thickness of slightly more than a tenth of an inch, bringing in hand-tools like a scraper only towards the end for fine adjustments. Now, he was working strictly by hand, discovering new muscles in his body and new responses in the wood as he tested various tools, including specialty spokeshaves and an Ibex finger plane, a miniature bronze plane so small that it disappeared when he closed his hand around it.

It was okay for him to experiment now with these tools while he still had a lot of material to remove. Later, the work would be riskier as he finished carving the top of the soundboard and began working on the underside to complete the arch. Even now he had to be cautious. He soon abandoned the mallet and chisel, returning to the gent's plane to avoid accidentally splitting off too much wood.

Many archtop builders drill depth guide-holes before removing material. This is the method suggested by Robert Benedetto in his book *Making an Archtop Guitar*, the main reference Robert was using. Robert elected not to do this, choosing to work by feel instead, occasionally using callipers to check depth as he went. I wondered if this was a wise decision, worrying as I did, about the danger of going too far and ruining the top we'd already invested considerable time in making. I mostly kept these concerns to myself, although I'm sure Robert picked up on my anxiety.

On the exterior he seemed confident and relaxed. When I asked him what he would do if he made a mistake, he just smiled and said he'd just have to start over if that happened.

It was hard for me to have the same confidence since, like a passenger in a car, I had no control and could only observe and imagine the twists and turns in the road.

Seven

MANZER AND METHENY

In 1964 when *A Hard Day's Night* was still on the movie screens, jazz guitar icon Pat Metheny got his first guitar and retreated to his bedroom in his Midwest family home in Lee's Summit, Missouri, where he began practising ten to twelve hours a day. He was eleven years old.

That single-minded focus, his talent, and that guitar (a Gibson ES-140 three-quarter-sized flat-top acoustic) started Metheny on a journey that saw him performing with A-list blues and jazz musicians in nearby Kansas City by age fourteen; teaching guitar at the University of Miami by age eighteen; moving on to teach at the prestigious Berklee College of Music when he was only nineteen; recording his first album *Bright Size Life* when he was twenty; and eventually winning (as of this writing) an unprecedented twenty Grammy awards in ten different categories, including "best jazz performance," "best rock instrumental performance," "best country instrumental performance" and "best jazz instrumental album by an individual or group."

Metheny calls himself a jazz guy but his musical

imagination has such reach, range and depth that he's difficult to categorize. He's received thirty-five Grammy nominations in twelve categories and has been named guitarist-of-the-year by prestigious magazine polls on a number of occasions. He's recorded thirty-seven albums and sold over twenty million records worldwide. He's a guitar superstar – some would say musical genius – unbounded by conventional definitions. He's also the best example of a guitarist who has worked closely with a luthier to find new vehicles of expression.

I met Metheny at his home in New York on a November morning in 2010. I was there to interview him for a documentary I'd pitched to *Inside the Music*, a CBC national radio program, about Canadian luthier Linda Manzer who'd built over twenty guitars for Metheny, contributing significantly to the development of his sound. (Entitled *Kindred Spirits: Linda Manzer's 30-Year Journey with Pat Metheny*, the documentary aired in August 2011 and is still available on the CBC website.)

I was vaguely aware of Manzer even before I wrote my first luthier article but her name came up in my interviews with Robert and other Vancouver Island guitar makers and I ended up contacting her to get a quote for the story. She was very accommodating and struck me as an interesting person. As I read newspaper and magazine articles about her, I began to realize that she had an amazing story to tell. She was often cast as a guitar-builder-to-the-stars since she'd made instruments for a number of famous musicians, but it was the Metheny story that interested me the most.

I was slated to meet Metheny at 10:30 am. I got there early and sat at a nearby cafe where I ordered a cup of tea and leafed through my notes, going over the questions I'd prepared the night before in my modest room at the Central Park Y. I hoped the tea would settle my stomach and the advanced preparation would focus my mind.

I had reason to be nervous. This was my first radio documentary. I'd recorded a successful interview two days before with Manzer at her workshop in Toronto, but my time with Metheny would be short and I had to get it right. There wouldn't be a second chance.

I'd interviewed famous musicians by phone for magazine and newspaper pieces, from Paddy Moloney of The Chieftains to Aaron Neville of the Neville Brothers, but to sit in person for an extended time with one of the most celebrated guitarists in the world, a musician I'd long admired, was going to be a joy but also a challenge. This was like interviewing Mark Knopfler, Eric Clapton or even a Beatle. This guy was a guitar god.

Two days earlier I'd arrived at Linda Manzer's house in Toronto's Cabbagetown, an historic downtown neighbourhood with Victorian three-storey brick houses and bare-limbed trees lining the streets, to find her dressed in jeans and a black T-shirt, sweeping her porch and shaking out her doormat in preparation for my visit. She was one of the best-known luthiers in the world because of her long association with Metheny and her work with other famous musicians, including Carlos Santana, Bruce Cockburn and Liona Boyd, but she was also a down-to-earth humble Canadian with a great sense of humour, qualities that had come across in the emails we'd exchanged.

She'd helped me arrange the meeting with Metheny by contacting his agent on my behalf. When we got the green light, she emailed a simple, "Pat is cool about doing this!! Can you come to NYC in November?" As we refined the details, subsequent emails had the same upbeat, friendly tone.

When I approached her Toronto house, the orange and brown leaves that littered her street crunching underfoot, I felt I already knew her and that our meeting was inevitable or somehow preordained.

With Metheny, on the other hand, I felt apprehension, probably because of his celebrity and the fact that I was in New York to interview him. This was daunting territory, the land of famous people.

Manzer had told me about a humorous celebrity encounter she'd had the one time she travelled to Metheny's apartment to deliver a guitar. She got on the elevator in the lobby with two men, one who was carrying a black-and-white polka dot box which attracted her attention. She looked over at them and realized one was Regis Philbin, the well-known game and talk-show host. She did a double take.

"In my mind I was scolding myself saying, 'Shit, I did a double take – now he knows I know who he is.' So being the good Canadian I did not want to bother him. So I actually didn't look at him again. I stood there frozen, looking straight ahead and dead quiet as they talked and I was completely nervous. It's a long elevator ride! About halfway up, he said, 'So ya play guitar do ya?' To which I answered something like, 'Actually I make them and I'm taking this one to a client in the building.' And "DING" the elevator door opened and I smiled at him and stepped out."

My own moment of awkwardness occurred even before I got on the elevator. Manzer had told me that I would encounter a concierge in the lobby, and so as I walked the one block from the cafe to the apartment building, I rehearsed in my head what I would say. I decided that it was probably most appropriate for me to refer to "Mr. Metheny," assuming there'd be considerable formality in the relationship between Metheny and the concierge. Wrong. When I approached the concierge at his desk, introduced myself and explained why I was there, he nodded, picked up the phone and said, "Pat, Rick Gibbs is here to see you."

Then I had to clarify with him what floor Metheny's apartment was on, even though it was contained within the address I was holding in my hand. He smiled patiently at my ignorance while I mumbled, "Ah, right," and turned my awkward provincial self towards the elevator bay.

Standing in front of Metheny's door, I triple-checked the number, took a deep breath and knocked. I didn't know who would open it. I imagined everyone from a personal assistant to a butler. But it was Metheny himself, dressed head-to-toe in faded blue denim, his iconic long frizzy hair tucked up under a backwards-facing denim ball cap. He smiled, reached out his hand and said, "Hi, I'm Pat," and we stepped inside.

Metheny's apartment was over forty floors up and the view of the city from the bank of windows along one wall of his home studio was impressive. His guitars, about thirty in all, hung on the other three walls with several more resting in a stand on the floor beside an L-shaped desk at the far end of the room.

A large Apple computer displaying the coloured tracks of a current recording project dominated the desk. Leaning against the inside corner of the "L" was his Gibson ES-175 electric archtop that he'd played for years but no longer toured with. I wondered what recording project he was working on, but I was too shy to ask, given that our interview had a specific purpose and our time was limited.

I was there to learn as much as I could about his creative relationship with Manzer – how the twenty or so guitars she'd built for him came to be, how those instruments shaped his music, and how their relationship had lasted for nearly thirty years. But first

I wanted to understand why he became a guitar player in the first place.

We set up for the interview in front of the desk. I sat almost knee-to-knee facing him. I'd secured a stool from a nearby piano and set up my digital recorder between us so I could monitor and control the recording.

Arming the record button, I started to explain my plan for the interview but Metheny cut me off.

"You know what – it's actually better if you don't tell me."

"You've done a lot of these," I said, trying to understand his motivation.

"Yes, and it's really better if it's spontaneous."

"Okay, I just need to do a sound check."

I put on my headphones and he jumped right in with a rapid "check, check, check, hello, hello, hello," followed by a "testing, testing, testing, one-two-three, testing." He'd obviously done this a thousand times and didn't need me to prompt him.

Linda Manzer had said that he worked extremely hard, accomplishing more in a day than anybody she knew. I was starting to see why. He was hyper-focused, concentrating fully on the task-at-hand and not wanting to waste a minute.

Satisfied with the sound in my headphones and the level on the meter, I glanced at my notes, took a breath and opened the conversation. "I'd like to start with where the guitar began for you."

Metheny jumped in as if he'd anticipated the

question. "I was backstage at a concert and one of the real odd unexpected benefits of ..."

He sounded great but there was a problem. He'd misunderstood my question. He was explaining how he met Linda Manzer and acquired his first Manzer guitar, not his first guitar ever.

What should I do? Feeling tense, I reacted too quickly. Instead of allowing him to finish and then rephrasing my question, something I would have done automatically in a magazine interview, I stopped him in mid-sentence, creating an awkward moment in which I had to explain what I wanted.

He adjusted and carried on.

"Well, I'm right at that age that's sort of the prime demographic of guitar players. I mean there seem to be millions of us that sometime in the mid-sixties after hearing the Beatles and acknowledging the sort of iconic place that the electric guitar found itself in as the symbol of an entire generation..."

I relaxed. He was launching into a perceptive and detailed explanation of how he came to take up the guitar, identifying both cultural and personal reasons for being attracted to the instrument. His answer was an interviewer's dream. Culturally he saw it as a phenomenon of the sixties and a pre-pubescent act of rebellion typical of kids his age. Personally it was a way for him to distinguish himself from his family – particularly his older brother Mike who was a trumpet prodigy.

"I was always being compared to Mike and the guitar served a few different purposes. It was a way of not being a trumpet player and it was not only a way for me to kind of remove myself from that whole idea of musical competition with my brother, but the guitar and later jazz was a way of sort of removing myself from everyone, which I realize now was kind of my goal. I always wanted to go off on my own and do my own thing and you know nobody in the town that I grew up in knew much about the guitar or jazz, so it was a double combination for me that was very powerful."

I was thrilled. I could already see a theme emerging in Manzer and Metheny's relationship that would serve the documentary well. In Toronto she'd explained to me that she came to the guitar, not as an act of rebellion but as an act of emulation. Like Metheny she'd been swept up by the sixties. Like Metheny, the Beatles had been the trigger.

"My mother is from England and so I was in England when they were just hitting the world by storm," Manzer had said, "and I came back with a little magazine with a picture of the Beatles on the back and I told all my friends in grade five that 'these guys are going to be the next big thing,' and so sure enough I was right – had my finger on the pulse – and I formed my first band which was called the Moptops…"

As Manzer told me that story, she gestured a lot and laughed at her so-called prescience, at the idea of young kids imitating the Beatles with mock guitars and a cardboard drum kit, and at the irony of one particular episode.

"I took a guitar – my brother reminded me of this – this is my first actual interaction with a guitar, which should have been a hint that I was going to be a builder and not a player. I took a guitar and because John Lennon had a Rickenbacker, which has got two pointy cutaways on it, I took a very normal guitar and I sawed it with my father's saw – really loud – right down the sides, and so I made it from fat to skinny, and then I put two papier mache horns on it and then I strung it back up again. What I neglected to do was to put the back on it. So what happens if you do that with a guitar, because the back holds all the tension, it bowed up like a bow and arrow and so the strings were now about a foot off the neck...it ended up in the corner and got thrown out with the garbage eventually but that was my first adventure into guitar-making."

I'd also learned from Manzer that 1974 was a pivotal year in her life. She'd become a folksinger and was studying at an art college in eastern Canada. She'd planted trees in northern Ontario and worked as a telephone operator. Like the rest of us – like Robert and me and hundreds of thousands of others of our generation – she was accumulating experiences and trying to find her path in life.

"I was not a really good folksinger, I wasn't a good painter...the thing that seemed to combine them all

59

was making guitars – that really fascinated me."

She started looking for someone to teach her and soon heard about Jean-Claude Larrivée who had opened an acoustic guitar factory in Toronto in 1967.

"I phoned him and bugged him basically until he hired me because he wasn't accepting new apprentices and he especially didn't want a woman. He actually said on the phone, 'I'm a male chauvinist pig.' As he was saying that, I could hear his wife laughing in the background, and I thought if she's laughing, he's not as bad as he thinks he is, and so I said those words that ring forever for me – 'I don't care if you don't care'– being the great feminist I was in 1974 – and so he tried me and it worked out. It ended up being an incredible experience and I was the only woman there for years and the guys were great. That's where I got my start in guitar-building."

Her start in instrument building had actually come a few years earlier when she was in high school and saw Joni Mitchell perform with a dulcimer at the Mariposa Folk Festival.

"I loved how simple it was…that it was just three or four strings. I went to the Toronto Folklore Centre to buy one. It was one hundred and fifty dollars, which I didn't have, so the storeowner talked me into buying a kit, which was half the price. I was sure I couldn't do it – we sat on the steps arguing about it and he finally talked me into to it – and so I went home with this kit and although I had no tools, I assembled it…the magic of it when you first put the strings on it…it was just this magic moment that I'd created this living musical instrument…it took me years to figure out that's what I wanted to do for a full-time job but that was the beginning."

When I asked Metheny what happened to him in 1974, he said by then he'd already been teaching for a year or two at the University of Miami and later at the Berklee College of Music in Boston. The Miami story, as recounted in an online interview I'd read, was particularly interesting because he'd gone there as a student out of high school on a scholarship after the dean happened to see him perform in Kansas City. But when he got to the university he realized he was completely out of his depth academically. He'd almost failed high school because he spent every waking moment playing and practising guitar. It was so bad his parents had taken away his guitar for a time. When he confessed his problem to the dean, the music department offered him a teaching post because he was already such an accomplished player and they were just opening up new electric guitar classes.

He explained to me that a lot more happened in 1974 besides the teaching. That was the year that jazz great Gary Burton invited him to join his band and he began touring internationally. It was also the year ECM Records invited him to record his first album. And most important in terms of his future relationship with Linda Manzer, 1973 and 1974 were the years he experimented with electronic equipment and became the first jazz guitarist to create a chorused sound that others would imitate. He was just emerging from his teens but already was an experimenter and innovator and was on a path that would eventually connect him with Linda Manzer.

Eight

VOWS OF POVERTY, VISIONS OF SUCCESS

Handcrafted guitars are expensive but the luthiers who build them do so for love, not money. Like musicians, many of them work at or below the poverty line to pursue their passion. It can take a builder a hundred or more hours to construct a flat-top guitar that might sell for three or four thousand dollars. Even if it sells for six thousand dollars as Robert's flat-tops typically do, by the time you factor in the cost of materials, a workshop, discussions with clients, and all the other time, energy and money demands of running a business, the hourly wage can be low. One young luthier I know turned to repair work after realizing he was earning less than ten dollars an hour building guitars. He now declines most guitar-building commissions because repair work pays so much better – an unfortunate development given his talent. Fortunately builders like Robert find ways to carry on.

Linda Manzer is in a different category now, a category where her instruments sell for ten thousand dollars or more, but it wasn't always so. She began her guitar-building career in her twenties, working in the Larrivée guitar factory first in Toronto and later in Victoria. The job provided a modest income and a valuable apprenticeship. Manzer reckons that in the time she was with Larrivée they built fifteen hundred guitars. As she puts it, she got to see "the good, the bad and the ugly." In other words she learned what worked and what didn't in guitar design and construction. She credits Larrivée with giving her "incredible training" and teaching her "great efficiency" but says, "like a baby bird" she needed to leave the nest.

"After three and a half years, he'd tripled his work force, we'd moved from Toronto to Victoria – he was going towards where he is now, which is a factory. When I started, there were about five us. There was a handful of people, we were friends, we would work late – it was just like a family."

"When he moved to Victoria, I think something in him changed, where he decided he just wanted to go for it and compete on the world-stage of making a lot of guitars and making a lot of money, which I absolutely understand now, but at the time I didn't like the idea at all. I didn't want to mass produce... I wanted to make handmade guitars and design them... so I came back here [Toronto] and I knuckled down and I worked and worked and worked and that's really what I needed to do."

Launching her own business meant a drastic reduction in income. "I was quite poor. I was skinny, I mean literally I didn't eat, but you know I went into guitar-making because I loved it. Although now I can sell my guitars for a lot of money, it was never about the money, that just happened later. It was kind of like signing an oath of poverty to be a guitar maker. It was always about the passion."

When Manzer moved back to Toronto, she went from working in a spacious machine-filled studio to sharing a hand-tool-equipped-only workshop above a pool hall on College Street with Michael Shriner, a lute maker. Shriner and Manzer were so poor they couldn't afford power tools even if they'd wanted them. But in the year or so she shared the shop, she got a valuable education in the use of hand tools and learned a lot about instrument making, new skills that augmented what she'd already learned from Larrivée.

Manzer's break came when she met Pat Metheny. By then she had her own workshop, had started selling guitars (including one to Carlos Santana), and had an apprentice, but she encountered a lot of discrimination because she was a woman in a mostly male trade. Potential clients wouldn't buy her guitars because they were built "by a girl" and they doubted her ability regardless of what their ears might be telling them about the quality of her instruments.

She was already a big Metheny fan, having first seen him perform with Joni Mitchell in 1979. "It was an outdoor venue and I had travelled with a bunch of musicians across the border to Detroit. We were outside and she was playing with this new band...she was playing "Amelia"…in the middle of the song this man steps forward. I'm way up in the middle of the back and it's dark and I've been hanging around with my friends digging Joni Mitchell. He stepped forward and he played a solo. About three notes in my world changed. It's like his music went right to my core…from those first few notes my life changed…from that moment on I sought out his music and he was the guy for me. He was the most incredible musician I'd ever heard."

Manzer saw him perform with his own band in Japan in 1981 and once again was blown away. Later that year he came to Toronto. She took a chance and sent a note backstage telling him she was a fan and guitar-builder and wondered if he'd like to come to her shop for tea the next day.

"I didn't know if I'd get an answer, and I was standing in front of the hall after he performed, and the tour manager came out and grabbed me and said, 'Pat wants to talk to you,' and I was standing with about fifty people and I went 'yikes!' and went down into the bowels of Convocation Hall and met Pat and he was just lovely and wonderful and warm, and we exchanged phone numbers and it was all vague."

Manzer carried on with the story. "Pat's drummer Danny Gotlieb and Peter, who was my apprentice at the time from Denmark, were watching the two of us talk and [one of them] said, 'This is stupid – why don't you guys go and grab some guitars.' So Pat and I looked at each other and said, 'Okay,' and so Peter and I ran back to my shop, grabbed a couple of guitars, met Danny and Pat in the hotel room, and stayed up until three o'clock in the morning. Pat played pretty much the whole concert over again on two of my guitars, sitting on the double beds – the four of us sat there – and at the end he said, 'Yeah, I'd like to buy one.' Of course I was through the moon..."

Manzer credits Metheny with changing the course of her career and her life. He was such a well-known guitarist that doubters finally had to recognize her ability and become believers.

Metheny says he'd already encountered numerous guitar-builders when he met Manzer. Typically they'd come to his sound checks to get him to try out their instruments. At that time he owned just a few guitars which he considered functional. He'd play the builders' guitars and acknowledge their quality but in the end would thank them and tell them he didn't really need another instrument.

It was different when Manzer showed up. "With Linda there was this instant recognition that this instrument was on an entirely different level. My first reaction to it was that it was not unlike the feeling that I have...when I sit down at a great German Steinway. It's incredible. It's just an unbelievable instrument. This was really the first time I'd ever felt that from a steel-string acoustic guitar. It felt like a Steinway to me. There was this incredible balance from the bottom to the top and this evenness that's incredibly elusive that she'd totally nailed. And after all this parade of guitar-makers had come over the years, it was the first time I said, 'I want to get this – I want this.'"

Manzer became in Metheny's words, "an ally" through which he could stretch his musical horizons and discover all that the guitar could be, demonstrating how important the instrument maker is in the music making process.

The first guitar she built for him was a steel string acoustic flat-top, an instrument he dubbed the 'Linda 6.' It became his mainstay acoustic instrument, accompanying him on his many world tours. I saw the guitar up close when I interviewed him and could see the wear – the scrapes, the scratches, the dings, the patches – that indicated it had been played as he put it " a lot." He said that's the way a guitar should look. He had little time for polished and babied instruments. To them they were meant to be played: tools to make music, not museum pieces to collect.

Manzer went on to build other conventional guitars for him, such as a nylon string acoustic and an archtop, but in response to his creative desires she also created unusual instruments like a sitar guitar and the most unique of all, the forty-two string 'Pikasso,' a harp guitar that took months to complete and was an engineering marvel.

One of Metheny's most popular albums is *Beyond the Missouri Sky*, a duo album recorded with bassist Charlie Haden. It's sold hundreds of thousands of copies worldwide. People play it at weddings and funerals. Metheny calls it, among other things, "the ultimate Manzer guitar demo album." He said it clearly represents the sound of her instruments because all the key guitars are there: the Linda 6, the sitar guitar, the nylon string guitar, the Pikasso, and so on.

Manzer told me the first time she heard it, she sat in the dark and cried.

I didn't ask her this question but I imagine that her tears were a response not only to the beauty of the music but also to the full realization of what her years of inspiration and dedication had wrought.

It is an album for the ages, a realization of the remarkable relationship between a great guitar maker and a great guitar player.

Nine

PASSIONS

Robert also chose to follow his heart, not his pocketbook, when he became a guitar builder. His work as an architectural designer and project manager paid well enough, but early morning phone calls, impossible deadlines, and the demands of clients took their toll, and in his forties he began imagining a less stressful life more in tune with his values.

Over his years as a musician, he'd met guitar makers and admired their skills but couldn't see how he could become one himself. One of the builders he met was Mike Jones, Jean Larrivée's brother-in-law, who'd worked in the Larrivée factory when it was located in Victoria. Robert wanted to take lessons from Jones, but at that time he didn't have the money to pay for them. Years later, through sheer serendipity, Jones showed up as a carpenter on one of the projects Robert was managing. The time was right and Jones agreed to teach him.

Robert's first instrument took two years of part-time work to finish but he completed the second in less than three months. He built it in the spring of 1997 and sold it that summer. He then quickly built two more.

In 1998, still a fledgling guitar builder, he met Eric Schoenberg at a guitar camp in Washington State. Schoenberg is the noted American fingerstyle guitarist and guitar designer who spent years persuading the Martin Guitar Company to re-introduce the Orchestra Model (OM) guitar, an instrument Martin introduced in 1929 but discontinued in 1934. He believed the early OMs were the best fingerstyle instruments available and eventually encouraged the Martin custom factory to build a few in the late sixties and early seventies. In the eighties, working with luthier Dana Bourgeois, he finally persuaded them to reintroduce OMs into their regular product line with some improvements he and Bourgeois had made to the original design. Today the OM is a standard part of the product lines of most major flat-top guitar manufacturers, and so his impact was significant.

Schoenberg worked with a number of luthiers over the years designing guitars under his own name for sale in his store. When Robert met him, he was looking for a new collaborator to build instruments for his shop in Tiburon, California. He liked Robert's work and invited him to become one of his builders. It took a year for Robert to produce an instrument that Schoenberg approved of – getting the dimensions and feel of the neck right, developing lightweight building techniques that would produce the best sound, perfecting all the details that go

into guitar construction to Schoenberg's expectations –
but soon Robert was shipping several guitars a year to
California as well as selling internationally under his
own name.

When I met him he'd already made about fifty
guitars that were noteworthy for their playability, light
weight and tone. About forty percent of his orders came
from Schoenberg, a major testament to Robert's skill,
given Schoenberg's profile and reputation for expecting
a lot of his builders.

As well, he'd exhibited his guitars at the Healdsburg
Festival, a juried acoustic guitar show that sees only a
hundred or so exhibitors selected from as many as a
thousand hopefuls. He'd also exhibited at the Montreal
Guitar Show, a similarly prestigious event for the best
guitar builders in the world.

He'd found a way to live the life he imagined.

I taught high school for twenty-five years, often yearn-
ing to be a writer. It wasn't until my illness surfaced and
its symptoms forced me to stop teaching, that I turned
to writing as my main professional activity, albeit part
time.

I enjoyed many aspects of teaching – being around
young people with their boundless energy and talent;
working with dedicated colleagues I liked and admired;
playing in various streams of knowledge – but it was
a profession that wore me down with its sixty-hour
weeks and endless bouts of marking (I taught English

and writing) that extended into the evenings, weekends and holidays. It was only in the summer that I was truly free, but by then I craved physical activity to counter the long hours spent sitting at a desk marking inexpert writing. (The Canadian author Robertson Davies, who taught university, once likened marking student writing to listening to bad music).

I channeled my writing desires into extra-curricular activities. Teaching in two schools in the course of my career, I started two student newspapers, developed an annual writers workshop in Vancouver attended by high school students from all over the Lower Mainland, and organized, with a local writer, a reading series in Victoria that gave talented kids the opportunity to read their own work alongside famous Canadian authors.

I coached debating, directed plays, and organized and supported outdoor activities like backpacking and rock-climbing. These pursuits gave me the chance to indulge my passions, while giving kids the opportunity to discover theirs. They formed the most enjoyable and fulfilling part of my teaching career. But they did take me away from writing.

Susan Ellenton, Robert's partner of thirty years, has some interesting thoughts about what it takes to be a self-employed artist. She's an accomplished silver artisan who has also worked as a visual artist, toured internationally as a singer-songwriter, and written musicals that have toured to Japan and the Smithsonian. Recently she wrote, "Our way of life – as two self-employed artisans – has evolved through a complex of choices, injuries, aptitudes, good fortune, flexibility, and ongoing conversations about our core values. Most of all, I think, it comes of choosing to trust."

Susan wasn't specific about whether the trust was tied to a particular belief system or the result of a general faith in the universe unfolding as it should – I suspect the latter – but she and Robert seemed to feel that opportunities would arise and their basic needs would be met if they followed their hearts and lived a life governed by their core values rather than the dictates of convention.

She didn't specify those values but I could see them in the way they lived their lives. My overarching impression was that they lived more consciously than most, focussing on a life of balance, quality and creativity.

When Robert and I were in his workshop, I sometimes thought of Robert Pirsig's *Zen and the Art of Motorcycle Maintenance*, a philosophical novel that explores notions of quality and the tension between romantic and classic views of thinking in the context of a seventeen-day motorcycle journey from Minnesota to Northern California. Like one of the characters in the book, Robert was a romantic who trusted that things would work out as they should, but he also had a rational, scientific way of being that came through in his work.

If, like the narrator of Pirsig's novel, he had owned

a motorcycle, he would have known its inner workings and had the tools to repair it. But he wasn't interested in vehicles. His was the world of stringed instruments and he approached the building of them as both an artist and a scientist. He worked by intuition and measurement, crafting beautiful objects in the process.

Meeting people like Robert and Susan allowed me to reflect on the value of following one's passions. Doing creative work they love in workspaces they have designed, artisans like Robert and Susan live purposeful lives that have fewer compromises than most of us put up with in the conventional workforce.

Robert's work schedule alone demonstrated his freedom. He rose when he woke up naturally and walked the hundred or so feet from his home to his workshop around ten each morning. He stopped for lunch at one or two in the afternoon, returning to the house where he and Susan sat in their kitchen and ate a leisurely lunch and sipped tea before returning to work for a couple of hours in the afternoon.

There were compromises. Robert sometimes worked in the evening teaching others to build guitars as a way of supplementing his income and advancing his practice, and so his schedule wasn't entirely his own. And the hassles of owning a small independent business were bound to crop up – the unhappy customer, the client who drops by and talks your ear off when all you want to do is carry on with your work, the financial concerns that might arise from an inconsistent income.

But when your vocation is your occupation, when work is engaging, when creativity defines most of what you do, you get to operate with a level of satisfaction not everyone achieves in their working lives. I've experienced some of that as a writer and even had moments as a teacher but I inevitably found myself envying their life and admiring the happy combination of talent, opportunity and flexibility that had made it possible.

With our archtop project I was getting to enjoy Robert's love of guitar building vicariously, while following my own dream of writing a creative non-fiction book. But I often wondered if I would get to see the project through to completion.

There were days I would arrive in the workshop tired from the chronic insomnia inflicted by the symptoms of my illness. The fatigue would usually fade as I became absorbed in our work, but the symptoms were a constant reminder of what a close writer friend who lost his sixteen-year-old son to cancer calls "the big black door."

When you get a serious illness, particularly one that involves the C-word (cancer, not chronic) you do a lot of second guessing. If only you'd eaten differently, exercised more regularly or pursued your passions earlier in life things might have been different. Self crticism might be justified if you found yourself with lung cancer after a life of smoking but most of the time there's no clear connection between individual behaviour and a serious illness.

The tendency to question ourselves is encouraged by a New Age ethic that believes in the power of magical thinking. There are people who think that parking spots are gifts from the universe that will appear through a positive mindset. These same people (when they are healthy) think that illness won't strike them as long as they eat their veggies and bounce happy thoughts around in their heads. They have little respect for the randomness of the universe and the precarious nature of human existence. I was like that myself at one time.

A close friend of mine, a poet, nearly died when an undetected cancer of the uterus led to major hemorrhaging. Learning of the illness, an acquaintance said, "Really? You don't seem to be the cancer type."

The cancer type. More faulty New Age thinking. People of all ages, outlooks and stations get major illnesses, including cancer. They may be smart, eat well, exercise, and be as happy as anybody can be – but still it happens. Young babies get cancer as do children and teenagers with good families, happy outlooks and strong spirits.

Why? I fear the answer amongst the New Age types will be 'karma,' an explanation I once embraced but find increasingly difficult to accept.

Many years ago I had a small patch of skin cancer on my forearm that fortunately was easily treated. I remember questioning the cause with my dermatologist. "It could just be random, you know," he said. Somehow that scientific view that recognized the tendency towards disorder in the universe was liberating.

Sometimes we survive brushes with entropy, sometimes we don't. We may go suddenly like a young bird against a window pane or slowly like an old frog sinking into the depths of a winter pond. We have some control through the way we live our lives, and science may eventually unlock genetic secrets that transform our relationship with illness, but ultimately we are as subject to the laws of nature as the ant or the oak tree. Things are born, they live for a time and then they die. That is life – at least the relative aspect of it that we experience most directly. We can only accept it for what it is.

I like to think that our consciousness – or some aspect of our spirit – is immortal but even that remains to be seen. As Shakespeare points out in *Hamlet*, no traveller returns from the "undiscovered country" and so we are left to wonder at the mystery of it all.

As for the archtop project, I was grateful that I was surviving and getting to witness the gradual realization of my dream.

The thing to do in guitar making as in life is to keep the cup half full and carry on.

Ten

FEEL AND TOUCH

A few days after Robert began carving the top, I arrived at his shop to find him elbow-deep in wood shavings. The rough carving finished, he'd moved the operation to the desk by the window, where he sat in his padded office chair with the top clamped to the desktop.

"I really like having the bright natural light to work with – I feel like I can see the shape so much better," he explained as he showed off his work and demonstrated how his unique clamping system functioned.

The system was so ingenious it interested me almost more than the progress on the top. He'd outlined an area on the desk with narrow strips of neoprene that stuck to the surface. Within that area a small hole connected to clear tubing under the desk ran through the exterior wall to an electric pump outside. Laying the soundboard atop the neoprene strips, he started the pump and the suction created within the sealed area held the top firmly in place. I was getting more insight into the practical imagination of a luthier.

The arch was now discernible. I ran my hand top-to-bottom and side-to-side, feeling the curves Robert had carved using only a chisel, a small plane, a spokeshave, and a scraper. I was surprised by how smooth and symmetrical the surface felt even though he'd done little measuring and used no sandpaper.

He explained that the work was a blend of precise measurement and intuition, adding that he had an internalized sense of what he wanted the curve to be, an ability to visualize that presumably came not only from researching archtop design but also from handling many instruments over the years.

He also had a romantic, almost mystical notion of how the process worked. "I think the piece of wood tells you what it wants to be," he said, explaining that each piece behaved differently under his tools. "If you are paying attention you get informed."

Robert spoke more like an artist than a craftsman. I'd read that Henry Moore, best known for his massive stone sculptures, also worked in wood and ascribed to it qualities not found in stone: "Wood is alive and warm and gives a sense of growth. Wood is a living and natural material. How much easier it is to open out wood forms than stone forms," he'd said when speaking about a reclining figure he'd "found" in a piece of elm long before he was able create it in stone.

Ross A. Laird, a west coast writer and woodworker, takes this notion further in his excellent book *Grain of Truth: The Ancient Lessons of Craft*.

"The curious thing about wood is that it does not

allow me to give up. It cajoles and prods, it demands that I keep my end of the bargain and bring out its hidden forms. At times it even taunts me, this ancient material possessed of its own craftiness. I'm not exactly sure how the wood makes its demands – saying that it speaks is only a shorthand for something more elusive and mysterious."

Robert didn't use anthropomorphism to explain his connection with wood but clearly he thought along the same lines. And it was apparent that hand tools helped create the relationship. Robert had told me about a luthier in the United States who used them exclusively, and indeed I'd met a builder in Victoria – Marcus Dominelli, a well-regarded classical guitar builder – who took great pride in crafting his guitars almost completely by hand, avoiding the use of jigs and machines whenever possible. He believed that to build a good guitar he had to handle the wood frequently.

I remembered taking woodworking classes in high school and spending a whole term in grade nine building a small wooden tray out of yellow cedar and black walnut. We used only back saws, mitre boxes, hammers, gouges, chisels, and sandpaper. Power tools were not permitted. I recall growing impatient with how long it took to complete such a small project, but now I could see the pedagogical wisdom of a hand-tools-only approach.

Laird certainly dislikes power tools. "They are indifferent to the quality of my work," he writes, "cutting without regard for the beauty and diversity of the materials. Hand tools, conversely, will purr and cough and shout. They change with the way I work, adapt themselves to the materials, remind me of their music at every turn. Pick up a well used and loved plane, one with a history of being cared for, and see how it skates incisively across the grain…listen to the distinctive whisper it makes as shavings spiral smoothly from its throat. Those shavings are the individual notes a plane makes in its song."

Hand tools do create a more intimate experience because they give the builder the means and time to actually feel the wood under the tool. And they are safer, although for years I had a small jagged scar on my left hand near the thumb where a back saw slipped when I was cutting a piece of wood in that same grade nine woodworking class. The scar has finally faded, but the memory lives on. I'm still very careful whenever I use a handsaw of any kind.

I was fortunate. The next year in grade ten, a classmate – a guitarist as it happens – cut off two fingers on a table saw. (We didn't use blade guards in those days.) I still remember him standing white-faced, holding his injured hand above his head with blood running down his wrist and dripping onto the concrete floor.

Fortunately the shop teacher acted quickly. He sent a kid to get a glass and some ice from the nearby home economics room, and picked up the fingers with a clean handkerchief, depositing them on the ice before rushing the victim down to the office and off to the hospital. The digits were reattached and it wasn't long before the kid could once again play his electric guitar.

Linda Manzer confessed to me that she's afraid of power tools, having sliced off the fleshy tips of a couple of fingers herself on a joiner over a decade ago. The experience was so traumatic she banished the tool to the far corner of her workshop.

"Yeah, that hurt," she laughed when she told me about the incident. "I went to the emergency ward and got eight stitches in each finger so I lost the fleshy part of those two fingers. But what's really good – you've got to be positive about this – it's turned into a very valuable wood-tapping tool."

Manzer demonstrated as she spoke, picking up a guitar-in-progress and tapping on the back – first with a regular finger and then with one of her damaged digits. The difference was subtle to my untrained ear but she assured me she could hear it clearly.

"So what are you listening for when you tap?"

"Sustain…mostly I listen for sustain because if it's dead that means you have to take more wood off, or conversely if it's dead, you've taken too much wood off. It sort of gets floppy. I figure once it's sounding like a bell – bing, bing, bing – and then when it starts to go soft and thuddy then I know I've taken a little too much off – which is actually not a bad thing because then I glue braces on and that adds more mass which adds more sustain; so I usually sand my guitar tops to where they just go off that perfect bell-like tone and then I know, because I'm adding struts or lacquer, that it'll pull back in again."

Manzer was explaining the process of "tap tuning" first developed by violin-builders in the late sixteenth century, refined by Stradivari in the seventeenth century and adapted to guitar and mandolin building by Lloyd Loar in the early twentieth century.

As the builder removes wood from the soundboard, she occasionally stops to hold it by her ear with one hand while tapping with the other to detect the pitch and degree of sustain. If the top is too thick, the note will be dead; too thin and it will get "thuddy". The builder is seeking a sweet spot, an ideal point where the tone is sustained and bell-like. Lloyd Loar, more acoustical engineer than builder, actually wanted the tops of his instruments tuned to specific notes, believing that was ideal. When Robert demonstrated tap-tuning to me, he didn't seek a specific pitch but rather a quality that I had trouble detecting but that an experienced builder gets to know through practice. The goal was to make the top as lively and responsive as possible without it getting so thin that it would fail.

Manzer explained this as she demonstrated her tapping finger: "The trick with making a musical instrument is to make it as strong as possible but also as light as possible so it will sustain and move. You want the wood to move because it's pushing the air inside the guitar, so you want it to be as sensitive but as a strong as possible."

For practical reasons Manzer has forced herself to get used to the noise and violence of her power tools but is much happier working with planes and chisels and scrapers. Robert is like this, too, and when he must use a power tool, he's selective. He seldom uses his table saw, preferring the more gentlemanly bandsaw, which he considers safer.

Laird shares his view: "Unlike my table saw with its voracious roaring appetite, the bandsaw is modest and restrained...because its blade is strung tight like a musical string, there is music to the work when things go well... problems with the cut can immediately be detected in the landscape of the sound."

Having used a bandsaw and table saw myself, I can appreciate the difference. The bandsaw starts with a surging jolt but quickly settles into a singing hum. The teeth are small, the blade thin and narrow. It's easy to keep the fingers away and ease the wood in for the cut. If the wood wanders off course or the blade twists slightly, the operator can pull back and make a slight correction with little damage. Try that with a screaming table saw and you'll butcher the cut or jam the wood against the rip fence, risking fingers as you try to free it.

As Robert worked on the top, he made short fast strokes with the Ibex finger plane, creating shallow grooves in the wood. Periodically he switched to the spokeshave, a small metal tool with slender handles and a fine blade, a kind of plane-in-reverse that in its crude stone form was first used in prehistoric times. He pulled it towards him with both long and short strokes to smooth the grooves created by the plane.

He occasionally stopped, bent over, and in the bright window-light looked closely at the arch he was shaping and refining, running  his fingers over the surface and checking for uniformity and symmetry. If he detected a bump or rise, he brought the finger plane or spokeshave to bear on that spot, removing just enough material to smooth it out.

He also checked the thickness with a pair of calipers, measuring now and then to be certain he hadn't gone beyond three-sixteenths of an inch. At some points he had reached the limit, at others, the wood was still too thick and he had more material to remove.

One area of concern was where the neck would join the body. Should that area be perfectly flat or should it rise gently? He was still figuring that out. "I like the way the shape evolves, how my thinking changes," he said, as the ribbons of wood piled higher on his desktop.

Eleven

THE FACTORY VERSUS THE WORKSHOP

I'm taking a virtual video tour of the Gibson guitar factory, trying to understand better the differences between factory produced and handcrafted guitars. Gibson is the company that gave birth to the archtop and so it seems only right that I should begin my investigation here. But we're not in Kalamazoo where it all started. The company left that factory behind in 1984 and moved to Nashville, Tennessee, leaving the original operation in the hands of a group of employees who formed the employee-owned Heritage Guitar Company, which is still producing instruments on old Gibson equipment.

It may not be the original factory but it is the company that invented the L-5, the ES-150, and the ES-175 – iconic archtops in the history of jazz. This is their solid body electric guitar factory – acoustic guitars are made in Bozeman, Montana, and archtops in their custom factory in Nashville – but the processes will be similar.

We begin on the sidewalk in front of a big blue Gibson USA awning. We pass through the glass doors and make our way to the "rough mill," where guitars-to-be begin their journey. Pallets of stacked, kiln-dried dimensional lumber and rough-cut body and neck blanks clutter the polished concrete floor and line metal racks, reaching for the ceiling of the packed warehouse-like building.

It's hot and noisy. The tour guide shouts over the steady din of saws, fans, vacuum systems, joiners, planers, sanders, and clanking pneumatic machinery to make himself heard. Some of the workers wear shorts, all wear T-shirts. I think of Robert's quiet climate-controlled workshop that he built from the ground up with his own hands and where the usual sounds are the strokes of a finger plane or the scrape of a spokeshave. When a power tool does assault the air and demand the donning of ear protection, it's momentary – here the din is constant.

The view shifts to a worker manhandling ten-foot-long mahogany boards from a lumber pile onto the rollers of a planer. He runs each plank through to surface it before passing it off to another worker who crosscuts it into short body blanks that are then ripped in half lengthwise by a third worker who quickly grades, matches and marks the pieces before rapidly stacking them on a pallet.

I wonder about these fast-moving white-gloved, ear-plugged men. Do they ever trade jobs or do they have just one skill, one trick that they repeat day after day, month after month, year after year? Do they go home worn-out, discouraged, dreaming of a job that doesn't deaden them so much? I think of Robert thoughtfully fingering the billet halves used for the top of my guitar, turning them over and back again on his bench, noting their characteristics, discussing their grain and figure. There is soul in that work. Where is the soul here?

Now I'm watching a red-shirted worker wearing denim shorts and a backwards baseball cap glueing mahogany blanks together. He stacks three on edge on the pallet, grabs three more, runs them over the roller of a glue dispenser before turning back to the pallet and plunking them edge first onto the first three he left behind. Now he cradles all six in his arms and turns to a pneumatic clamping machine where he pitches them into a rack, lines them up, sets and tightens the metal clamps and sends them on their way as the machine rotates to the next rack that he'll empty and then fill with newly glued blanks. The tour guide marvels at how fast Red Shirt goes and how expert he is. "He's been doing this job for so long..." he intones, full of pride and amazement.

He's proud, too, that the machine can accommodate over a hundred glued blanks at one time and that by the time a new set cycles back around to Red Shirt for removal, the glue is dry enough for him to stack the glued pieces on a pallet ready for the next operation. I think of Robert's method – his little pot of hide glue heating up on the bench in his quiet shop, his strips of masking tape and the one clamp he used to be sure the blanks would seat properly.

Red Shirt, with his hissing, clanking machine "processes" hundreds of blanks in a day. He must dream body blanks all night long just as I dreamt stacks of flying paper when I worked in a paper mill when I was twenty years old. I stayed in that job for nine months before returning to university. I was never so glad to get back to a classroom.

Now we're watching a big Northwood five-head CNC machine process blanks that have been rough-cut to shape on a bandsaw. This hydra-headed metal monster is drilling, routing and shaping the bodies to their final dimensions and specifications with jerky robotic motions. With its computer chip brain, tooled turret head and pneumatic muscles, it can do a set of five blanks in five to ten minutes. That must be thirty to sixty guitar bodies an hour, as many as four hundred and eighty in a single day.

The camera cuts to a different area where workers sort pallets of mahogany neck blanks, stacking them for drying in a kiln before they'll be rough-cut on a bandsaw. From there they go to a clamping table where "peghead ears" designed to increase the width of the headstock are matched to each blank and glued on. Then it's on to the rotary profiler which further cuts and shapes them to size before workers pass them on to the gang drill station to have the headstocks drilled for the tuning machines that will eventually be installed. Then in a series of operations using various power tools, one worker profiles the headstocks, another cuts channels for the truss rods, a third installs the rods and glues in the wooden splines that hold the rods in place. (Here the tour guide explains that the Gibson Guitar Company invented the truss rod, a feature used now by virtually every steel string guitar company in the world).

We head to a different building where finer operations and final assembly will take place. We start at a pallet stacked with rosewood fingerboard blanks destined to be dried in a kiln. Once their moisture content is stabilized they'll go through various processes before being glued to the necks. One worker will radius them, another will load them into a machine that cuts the slots for the frets, a third will tap in and snip off the fret wire before placing the completed fingerboards in a pneumatic press that seats the frets firmly. Eventually these fingerboards will be glued to the necks and the necks attached to the bodies.

Hand operations, similar to ones that Robert completes in his shop, proliferate as the tasks get more specific and the guitars near completion. One worker glues in plastic fret board dots, another installs the fingerboard binding, yet another glues on the headstock veneer before a fourth glues the fingerboard to the neck. Hundreds of necks are completed every day and always the workers are aided by machines that accelerate pace. Always they are tied to one station and one task. Always they move quickly, efficiently. Machine time.

As I watch the tasks being completed, an irony strikes me – these workers are making instruments that facilitate individual expression but are ultimately mass-produced objects of the industrial age. Soul will have to come later – it's not part of the factory equation.

Before guitars were produced in factories they were built in the small workshops of the European craft guilds. During the Middle Ages serfs were land-bound, but townspeople had the freedom to choose their own careers. Some became traders and formed merchant guilds. Others made products and created craft guilds. The craft guilds offered a path of development from apprentice to journeyman to master, terms we still use today to describe levels of skill and experience amongst carpenters, electricians, plumbers and other tradespeople. A young person would study under a master until his work was good enough to qualify him for entrance to the guild. Later he might travel to other towns to further develop his skills – hence the term 'journeyman.' In time he could become a master craftsman. Our modern romantic notion of the solo artisan doing valuable work that he loves comes from this era.

The masters who ran the workshops were typically jacks-of-all-trades, building, teaching, buying raw materials, marketing their products and managing staff. Under the umbrella of the guild, they regulated working conditions, set wages and prices, and wielded enough political power to monopolize the trade of their products. To become a master craftsman or artisan was to become a master of your own fate to some degree. But as commerce expanded through the Middle Ages and into the Renaissance, the merchant guilds grew more powerful and sometimes absorbed the craft guilds. Craftsmen were excluded from the guilds and became mere wage earners. Even in the craft guilds that survived, masters began acting more like entrepreneurs looking for cheap labour than educators guiding the development of their charges.

Contributing to the breakdown was the increasing specialization and fragmentation of the crafts. When the guilds first appeared in the Middle Ages, a young person entering the woodworking trades might learn to be a carpenter who constructed houses, made cabinets and built furniture. In later periods woodworkers had to specialize, becoming a wood turner or maybe a cabinetmaker. Consequently a city that had thirty craft guilds during the Middle Ages might have as many as a hundred by the Renaissance. Large workshops brought the different specialities together under one roof and began producing multiple products. These large workshops hired waged workers to fulfill specific roles. Generalists became specialists. The seeds of the factory system were sewn.

The rise of these large workshops led to conflict between the guilds as workshops sought to expand their trade by producing goods that at one time would have been out of their realm of expertise. One such dispute flared up in the early eighteen hundreds between the

Cabinetmakers Guild and the Violin Makers Guild of Markneukirchen, a town in Saxony, Germany, near the Czech border.

Some members of the Cabinetmakers Guild – including Christian Friedrich Martin, the man who would emigrate to America and create the Martin Guitar Company – were building guitars. The Violin Makers Guild didn't like this, believing they were the true musical artisans, and so they tried to stop it. In 1826, they grew aggressive, denouncing the cabinetmaker guitar builders as "bunglers" and "mere mechanics." Seeking an injunction they asked, "Who is so stupid that he cannot see at a glance that a grandfather's armchair or a stool is no guitar, and such an article appearing amongst our instruments must look like Saul amongst the Prophets."

The Cabinet Makers countered by noting that the Violin Makers had no vested right in building guitars and that Martin, one of their star builders, had started as an apprentice and risen to the level of foreman in a factory of a noted violin and guitar maker in Vienna before returning to Markneukirchen. He might be in the Cabinetmakers Guild but he was a master instrument builder. The dispute took twenty years to settle (in favour of the cabinetmakers) but by then Martin had followed another builder, Heinrich Schatz, to New York where he opened a store, began building guitars and selling a variety of musical instruments. Eventually he would follow Schatz to Nazareth, Pennsylvania, and establish the Martin Guitar company and factory.

The Martin and Gibson stories illustrate the development of factory guitar building in North Amer-ica. Martin started because skilled immigrants sought new opportunities in a new land. Gibson began because a native son came up with new ideas that excited a group of local entrepreneurs. In both cases one-man workshops that catered to local musicians became larger workshops that traded regionally on developing reputations. Eventually they became small factories with waged employees who completed specific assembly line tasks, turning out more and more guitars every year. This is essentially the story of Gretsch, Fender, Epiphone, Godin, Larrivee and many other North American manufacturers that now serve an international market.

It's not the story of builders like Robert who strive to keep the artisan lifestyle alive in a world that rewards efficiency over quality and ships even the good factory jobs offshore to realize more profit.

The factory system has its place of course – not everybody can afford a handmade guitar – but it's in the workshops of the artisans that innovation takes place and the soul of the stringed instrument is kept alive.

Twelve

D'ANGELICO AND D'AQUISTO

One builder who steadfastly refused to go the manufacturing route was John D'Angelico, an icon in the world of archtop guitars. Born in New York City in 1905 to an immigrant family from Naples, D'Angelico apprenticed to his grand-uncle Raphael Ciani when he was only nine years old, taking over supervision of the business when he was eighteen after Ciani died. Working for his aunt, he continued producing violins, mandolins and guitars in a workshop that employed twelve to fifteen people. But he wasn't happy being an employee or a supervisor and so when he was twenty-seven he quit to open his own shop at 40 Kenmare Street on the Lower East Side. There he built archtop guitars patterned after the Gibson L-5.

Initially D'Angelico worked day and night to get his guitars out and his name known. Even though he was hand building them, he sold them at the same price as the factory-built Gibsons to ensure that he was competitive. Gradually his instruments became known for their acoustic and aesthetic quality and soon the top guitarists in the city were his clients. They often had specific functional or aesthetic requests and he was only too happy to grant them, working with each musician to produce a custom guitar.

D'Angelico started with a few employees but pared it down to just one, his assistant Vincent DiSerio. DiSerio began working with D'Angelico in 1932 when he was only twelve, performing various 'gopher' activities – sweeping floors, picking up tuners and taking necks to the engraver to have the D'Angelico name inscribed on the headstock.

After leaving the army at the end of WWII, DiSerio returned to the shop and began working on the guitars directly – drawing templates, cutting body and neck blanks, cutting and glueing on fingerboards – while D'Angelico continued to handle the more refined tasks like carving the tops and backs. Gradually DiSerio became intimately involved in designing and building D'Angelico's guitars, although he never did any of the carving, bending of the sides, or final shaping of the necks. He stayed with D'Angelico until 1959 when they had a falling out, apparently over D'Angelico's ongoing refusal to turn his workshop into a small factory so they could make more money.

In 1952 a seventeen-year-old named James D'Aquisto walked into D'Angelico's shop to check out his guitars. He'd heard about D'Angelico from a guitarist he'd met at a jam session who told him that all the best players in New York owned D'Angelicos. D'Aquisto recounted the story to Paul William Schmidt for his book *Acquired of the Angels: The Lives and Works of Master Guitar Makers John D'Angelico and James L. D'Aquisto.*

"So one day this new friend took me down to John's on a Saturday. John was finishing up an eighteen-inch New Yorker for Al Chenet...I saw the guitar and I flipped. John said, 'Would you like to try it?' So I sat down and he placed it in my lap; I played a chord and I couldn't believe it – it sounded like a piano. I'd never heard anything like that or ever thought a guitar was supposed to sound like that!"

D'Aquisto, who was working as a department store stock boy after leaving school without graduating, went to the shop every chance he got, taking along bridges, pickguards and other attachments he'd made at home to show D'Angelico.

D'Angelico noticed his interest and offered him a job, essentially the position DiSerio had held before the war – sweeping floors, picking up tuners and tailpieces, taking necks to the engraver, and so on. D'Aquisto leaped at the chance, and soon was secretly learning all the guitar making skills that DiSerio had picked up following the war. D'Angelico would leave the store every afternoon to hunt for interesting tools and gadgets in the hardware stores and machine shops of Manhattan. While he was out, DiSerio would teach D'Aquisto a skill and then sit and read the newspaper while D'Aquisto completed the work. They'd switch back to their normal roles before D'Angelico returned.

After the falling out between DiSerio and D'Angelico, D'Aquisto revealed to his boss all the skills he'd learned from DiSerio and expressed an interest in also doing the critical work of carving necks, tops and backs. Soon he was doing everything but designing and building the instruments on his own. He and D'Angelico grew into a powerful team, with D'Aquisto not only drawing all the knowledge he could from D'Angelico, a man he considered a master artist, but also upping the game by bringing his own vision and refined skill to the enterprise. Among other things, D'Aquisto brought more consistency to D'Angelico's process by creating templates and jigs for particular operations.

In the early sixties, as the two men worked closely together, D'Angelico's archtops reached a peak in sound quality and design, but D'Angelico, whose health had been failing with bouts of pneumonia and repeated heart attacks, died suddenly at the age of fifty-nine on September 1, 1964. D'Aquisto, who had grown very close to him, was devastated.

With the blessing of the family, D'Aquisto took over D'Angelico's business under his own name, eventually moving to Long Island. D'Aqusito went on to become the pre-eminent archtop builder of the twentieth century, in many ways surpassing his mentor. He died in 1995 also at the age of fifty-nine.

Today his archtops are highly valued (selling for as much as $500,000) and are considered the best ever built. Linda Manzer studied with him for a time and in the book *Blue Guitar* (Chronicle Books) by Ken Vose she describes what he was like.

"Working with him was an exhausting but magical experience. Although he was a man who loved lively discussion – very lively at times – sometimes he said more with his silence. I would watch him as he'd feel the weight and texture of each piece of wood before he would even tap it. After he felt acquainted with the wood, he'd silently make a decision about how it would interact with the other woods. Then the work began. As he carved the tops and backs, he would work the wood with confidence. One always had the feeling he knew exactly where he was going with each guitar."

D'Aquisto began by producing classic archtop guitars modeled after D'Angelico's instruments, but as we'll see, he eventually broke free and towards the end of his life became a major innovator.

D'Angelico began by imitating a factory-made guitar, the Lloyd-Loar-designed Gibson L-5. While that guitar itself is an iconic instrument that launched the modern era of the archtop, it's widely acknowledged that D'Angelico surpassed it both sonically and aesthetically with his designs.

First and foremost his guitars were musical tools built for musicians. They were so sonically refined they often staggered the musicians who, playing them for the first time, couldn't believe the rich, even sounds they were hearing from a guitar.

But he also made the guitar an art object by

introducing culturally significant design elements, such as stepped art deco pickguards, elaborate headstocks, and engraved tailpieces that took archtop guitar-making to new aesthetic heights.

D'Angelico and D'Aquisto could not have made such deep contributions to the art of guitar making if they'd turned their shops into factories. By choosing the path of the artist rather than the entrepreneur, they were free to explore, dream and inspire new generations of archtop builders.

Thirteen

INTOXICATION

Some guitarists constantly search for the perfect instrument, buying, selling and trading in the hopes that one day they'll find it. By the time our project started I'd owned and sold a dozen guitars in my quest.

Some players have bought and sold hundreds. Some own hundreds. Scott Chinery, a wealthy American collector, had over one thousand mostly vintage guitars by the time he died prematurely at age forty in 2000. A few years before his death, inspired by a guitar built for him by Jimmy D'Aquisto, he commissioned the building of a special collection of archtops by twenty-two of the best luthiers in the world. Each builder was given the same instructions – create an eighteen-inch (at the lower bout) acoustic archtop that is as traditional or contemporary as you like. The only stipulation – it must be coloured blue using a bottle of Ultra Blue Penetrating Stain #M 520 from Mohawk Finishing Products in Amsterdam, New York, the same stain that D'Aquisto had used for his instrument.

Chinery and D'Aquisto, in discussing the future of

the archtop guitar, had decided that one way to bring attention to a guitar they considered far more versatile than the much more popular flat-top, would be to create a contemporary version that in its aesthetics would embody modernity and thus put a lie to the notion that it was an instrument suitable only for old jazz tunes.

To make it really contemporary they considered purple and red but settled on blue, perhaps thinking about Picasso's famous 1903 painting "The Old Guitarist" from his "blue period" or the modernist poem inspired by that painting, "The Man with the Blue Guitar" by Wallace Stevens.

Whether it was the painting, the poem or just pure intuition that guided them, Chinery and D'Aquisto did catch the attention of guitarists and artists alike. The Blue Guitars became an exhibit at the Smithsonian in 1998 and helped take the modern hand-built guitar beyond craft to the stature of art.

Chinery's project inspired the aforementioned book *Blue Guitar*. Ken Vose quotes Chinery's thinking when he first conceived of the project.

"I had often thought that it would be neat to get all the great portrait painters together to interpret the same subject and then see the differences among them. So that's what I set out to do with The Blue Guitars. To get all the greatest builders together and have them interpret the same guitar, an eighteen-inch archtop, in the same color blue that Jimmy had used. All of these great luthiers saw this as a friendly competition, and as a result they went beyond anything they'd ever done. We ended up with a collection of the greatest archtop guitars ever made."

Linda Manzer was one of the builders invited by Chinery to participate in the Blue Guitar Project. In *Blue Guitar* we also learn about her thinking and approach.

She called her archtop "The Blue Absynthe," after the liqueur that was popular amongst French artists at the turn of the century. "I chose the name because like the eighteen-inch archtop, it's an intoxicating, mythical elixir."

She used European spruce, a favoured wood, for the top, and European maple for the back, sides and neck. The fingerboard, pick guard, tailpiece and bridge were all ebony as were the bindings. Manzer said her intention was to create elegance without flash.

The photo of the Blue Absynthe reveals a design that is at once traditional and contemporary. The f-holes are violin-like but have a smoother contemporary curve to them, while the pickguard has a step that recalls the art deco designs of the early New York archtops but is softened with a curve. The fingerboard inlays are rectangular like those found on early Gibson L-5s but are made more contemporary with angled breaks.

Chinery asked Manzer and a few other builders to include a sound port on the top (bass) side of the guitar, a design feature used by some contemporary luthiers to allow players to hear their instruments more clearly and to alter the sound by opening it up more. Manzer, who likes unusual challenges, decided to create a sliding door for her port to allow the player to fine tune the sound. (Robert and I discussed and eventually decided to include a small sound port on my guitar albeit without the sliding door). With the port open Manzer says the sound is more akin to a flat-top guitar and with it closed it has the projection of a traditional archtop.

She confessed to Vose that she wasn't always a fan of the archtop, something she'd told me as well. In the early part of her career, she thought they looked great but sounded too "chunky." When she received a grant to study archtop building with D'Aquisto at his Long Island studio, her thinking changed after she played one of his instruments. "I realized there was some real magic that I hadn't seen or heard before that moment. I was hooked."

Guitarists can be as attracted by the look, smell and feel of their instruments as by the sound. I still recall the beautiful smell of a Taylor 612C flat top guitar that I purchased in the 1990s but subsequently sold a few years later to help fund a trip to India. Every time I picked up that instrument I'd hold it to my nose before playing and inhale the woody, resin-like fragrance that emanated from the sound hole.

The ebony fretboard, the spruce top and the honey-coloured maple back and sides along with that scent created an object that I'm sure caused dopamine, the pleasure chemical in our brains, to flow abundantly.

105

Some theorize that an obsession with guitars and the desire to own many of them is a distinctly male thing. Women, it is said, are monogamous and stick to one guitar, while men wander and play the field – or so the theory goes. I'm not sure I agree, although guitars are sensual objects. Even the staid violin has been characterized historically as feminine in nature.

Beholding a beautiful guitar, whether factory or hand-built, certainly triggers an aesthetic response. I find myself captured by the sheer beauty and presence of the instrument.

Our word for this experience comes from the Greek word *aisthetikos*, meaning "pertaining to sense perception." In the eighteenth century the German philosopher Alexander Baumgarten coined the term *aesthetics* to try to explain our response to art, an experience based more on perception and feeling than on logic and thought.

More recently researchers have found that apprehending a work of art, whether a Monet or a Picasso, increases activity in the pleasure centres of the brain normally associated with romantic love. Blood flows to these areas as the level of dopamine rises, stimulating feelings of desire, love, and pleasure. So perhaps the theorists aren't so far off after all.

I was certainly hopeful that Robert's guitar would put an end to my philandering and that my search for the perfect guitar would be over. I wouldn't know for sure until I held the finished instrument and played it for the first time.

We were still a long way from that moment and I was still wondering if I'd even reach it. Lab tests showed my chronic illness continued to be stable but that didn't stop me from wondering.

Fourteen

THE MIDDLE WAY

Robert emailed to say he was ready to start the next phase of carving the top. He'd got the top side to where he wanted it and was now ready to finish the job by removing material from the still-flat underside.

I arrived to find him setting up his drill press with a most unusual attachment. Carving the harder-than-expected Sitka spruce with hand tools for hours had convinced him to adopt the method used by Bob Benedetto and many other archtop builders – he would drill a gridwork of holes to serve as depth guides and to remove some of the material before he started using his hand tools.

To do this job he'd fitted his drill press with a lacrosse ball screwed to the end of a short length of wooden dowel. The dowel fit into the clamp that normally held the drill press table. The hard rubber ball gave him a round surface that would accommodate the curves of the already-carved side as he moved the top around to drill the holes. Here was yet another example of Robert's practical imagination – where a tool didn't exist, invent one using everyday objects – although Robert acknowledged this particular device had been developed by his friend Jim Ham.

There was one problem. He needed two hands to move the top around on the ball as he drilled. He asked me to work the spoked handle of the drill press, bringing the spinning bit repeatedly down onto the underside of the top as he shifted it around to each new hole location. We had to drill hundreds of holes.

I told Robert I was nervous, given all the work he'd already put into carving the top. What if something went wrong and I went too deep or worse yet, drilled right through? He just smiled, glanced up at his wood supply still stacked on an overhead shelf, and said he'd just have to start again, adding that he'd checked the depth carefully a few times and set the stop on the drill press to prevent such a disaster from happening. I suspected he was becoming amused by my recurring anxiety.

I felt tension in my stomach as we prepared to drill the first hole. I brought the bit down slowly and grimaced slightly as it bit into the spruce, sending bits of wood flying across the pristine surface. I drilled the second hole with slightly more confidence. The third was easier still as I finally accepted that the bit wasn't going to chew through to the other side. Soon I was drilling with abandon and before long the whole underside was riddled with rows of holes that made it look like a giant guitar-shaped cheese grater.

The job done, Robert cleaned off the top and took it to his desk, securing it once again with his vacuum clamp, this time in a cradle he'd fashioned to accommodate the already-carved top side that would no longer lie flat.

He then donned a leather glove – he'd developed a blister on his thumb from all the carving of the top side – and set to work with the Ibex finger plane. The gridwork of  holes allowed the carving to go much faster because there was less material to remove and the depth was already predetermined. Before long, his clean desktop was deep with curled ribbons of wood. I left him to his work, pleased with the progress we were making.

The next time I visited Robert's shop, he'd finished the main carving of the underside. All that was left was to cut the f-holes and carve the final gradations that would produce a flexible top that would respond well to the vibrations of the strings. Too stiff and the guitar could end up sounding weak. Too flexible and the top could fail. As Linda Manzer had explained, this is the challenge of the luthier: to balance sensitivity with strength, to have the courage to go far enough and the wisdom to stop before it is too late, to tread what seemed to me a kind of Buddhist middle path that would produce the best possible result. There were life lessons in this carving.

Bob Benedetto in his book *Making an Archtop Guitar* (Centerstream Publishing), considered by many the contemporary bible of the craft, advocates working quietly and patiently without distractions and getting to know the wood intimately as the only way to learn and develop the skills needed to accomplish this task. His instructions suggest almost a meditative focus. (Note: in his book he refers to the top and bottom of the guitar body as "plates.")

"Begin with the roughly-carved top plate. Without distractions from a radio or people, handle the plate with both hands. With one hand located at the neckblock area and the other at the tailblock area, twist the plate one way and then the other. Next, hold the plate in both hands at the lower bout. Flex it one way and then the other. While holding the plate in one hand, pass the fingertips of the opposite hand across the outside of the plate and listen carefully to the tone produced. Check the tap tone. The objective is to become 'acquainted' with the plate. Repeat these steps over and over until you begin to feel the plate's stiffness, how it vibrates and the tone it produces. This is a learning process and not as easy as reading a ruler or caliper. Take your time, be patient, and go through the motions. It is the only way to learn and develop your skills."

Benedetto goes on to say that since this is not an exact science, it's difficult to describe exactly how flexible the plate should be or what particular tap tone pitch is appropriate at any given stage. A final tone of Bb may be optimal for one piece of wood while C may be best for another. The objective is to get a clear, sustained tone of some kind. Like Robert he seemed to think the wood itself would inform him through experience, intuition, and careful attention to the process.

Benedetto advocates adherence to specific measurements that vary only slightly, depending on the form of bracing that will be used. These braces will be glued to the underside of the top at a later stage to add strength and prevent the soundboard from failing under the strain of the tensioned strings pressing down on the bridge. They'll also act as tone bars to distribute the strings' vibrations to the soundboard. Usually two braces are employed, either running parallel down the length of the soundboard between the f-holes or cross-wise to form an X. More traditional archtops, taking their cue from the violin family, are built with parallel braces. Modern luthiers, who've experimented with various forms of flat-top bracing, often favour the X-brace, believing it adds warmth to the sound. Benedetto argues that parallel braces, because they provide better support, allow the top to be thinner, producing more volume and projection. X-braces, he says, make for a thicker-topped, quieter, more mellow sounding guitar. For the X-bracing that Robert was planning to use, the thinnest gradation of the soundboard would be one-eighth of an inch near the outside edge, gradually thickening to a quarter of an inch near the middle. If he were to employ parallel braces, the middle could be thinner at just three-sixteenths of an inch. (We later decided to go with parallel bracing).

While the details of the craft in the Benedetto book were mostly abstractions to me, I realized their substance when I got to hold the almost-finished top and marvel at the transformation our chunk of 'firewood' had undergone. In Robert's hands, through many hours of carving, that rough chunk of material had become a smooth, featherlight, gently arched soundboard ready to respond to every move of my fingers on the strings.

Robert invited me to hold it and try flexing it myself. I balanced it carefully in my hands, unwilling to test the flex for fear of cracking it. I did sniff it – there wasn't much scent from the Sitka spruce – and did look closely at the fine lines that comprised the grain. It really was a marvel, this skilfully shaped object that seemed almost light enough to float on air.

Later we would lay out and cut the f-holes, using a design that Robert had created after considering the many variations possible in the Benedetto book, from the relatively narrow Gibson L-5 shape to the wider, chunkier Epiphone Deluxe shape. He settled on a generous, well-balanced f-hole more akin to the Guild Artist shape, getting me to approve the design before we actually cut the top. I was happy to do so since he'd produced an elegant, simple design that appealed to my sensibility. No fancy curly-cues for me. This was to be a west-coast guitar and I wanted it to reflect a simple west-coast sensibility.

More important than the specific pattern was the placement of the f-holes between the centre-line of the bridge and the outer edge of the lower bout. Most people think that holes are cut in a guitar top to allow the sound to escape. I certainly did. Technically that's not quite correct. Their main purpose is to alter the vibratory nature of the soundboard. Cutting a hole or holes allows the top to vibrate more freely, thus producing more sound. The shape and placement of the holes changes the voice of the guitar and influences its ability to project.

F-holes are favoured on archtops because it's believed they produce a balanced sound in all registers, much as they do in a violin, viola or cello. The bass, mid-range, and treble notes ideally will come out equally rich and even. One register won't predominate over another.

Some archtops are built with round or oval holes. Indeed Orville Gibson's archtops were constructed this way, but once Lloyd Loar utilized the f-hole, round and oval holes largely disappeared, although some archtop builders have revived them either for aesthetic purposes or to produce a guitar that is closer to a flat-top in character. I own a Takamine J-15e archtop designed in 1981 for Ry Cooder that has a round soundhole. It's a big-bodied guitar that sounds more like a flat-top. Although it has parallel braces, it doesn't project very well because the top is thick and heavy. It seems to have been designed specifically to be amplified since it has a unique under-the-saddle pick-up peculiar to Takamine. It does sound good plugged in but has a very different character than most other archtops. I'm hard-pressed to hear much difference between it and a flat-top.

Benedetto notes that the area between the f-holes is the heart of the vibrating surface. If they're placed too close together the surface will be reduced, weakening the voice of the guitar. If the holes are too narrow, they will choke the voice, producing a weak sound, particularly in higher registers. Too wide, says Benedetto, and the guitar may have less projection.

Time would tell how our guitar would sound but increasingly I had faith that the result would be good.

Fifteen

BIG TREES

Conifers like Douglas fir, Western red cedar, hemlock and Sitka spruce dominate the Vancouver Island landscape where I live. Drive north on Highway 1 from my home in Victoria over the Malahat Highway to the town of Duncan and you'll see second-growth evergreen forests lining both sides of the highway and filling the hillsides that climb towards the mountainous central spine of the two-hundred-and-ninety-mile-long island. Head further north to Nanaimo, Parksville, Qualicum Beach, Courtenay, Campbell River, and Port Hardy, or turn west on Highway 4 at the mid-island point to Port Alberni and Tofino, and the effect is multiplied. Even with the hundred and fifty years of logging that has removed nearly ninety percent of the old growth trees from the Island and denuded many of its hillsides, the predominant effect is not of an emerald isle but of a dark green coniferous one, broken – from the road at least – only by ocean views, rock faces and the periodic settlements found in the valleys on the eastern side of the Island.

Take that drive on an autumn day and you'll notice something associated mainly with central and eastern Canada – the flaming yellow, orange and red hues of deciduous trees turning colour. While some of this effect is created by species such as red alder, black cottonwood and Pacific dogwood, two maple species are responsible for much of it. One is the vine maple (Acer circinatum), which sometimes reaches a height of sixty feet but more often grows as a leggy shrub or small tree under the dense canopy produced by the towering evergreens of the mixed temperate rain forest. The other is the Big Leaf maple (Acer macrophyllum), the largest maple tree in Canada, which can grow over a hundred feet tall and in the right conditions produce a crown nearly as wide, with large branches decorated by dinner-plate-sized leaves spreading in all directions.

Hike the damp forests of the Island in the fall and these huge leaves carpet the trails, while overhead, the giant moss and lichen-covered branches of their parent trees twist and turn against the blue sky. It's been said that if you could pile all the leaves of a Big Leaf maple on one side of a scale and all of the moss and lichen covering the trunk and limbs on the other, the latter would outweigh the former, particularly on older trees that support vast quantities of these epiphytic plants.

In the spring when the rain clouds disappear and the sun emerges, the newly sprouted leaves produce a dappled green canopy that deepens in colour and density as summer approaches, the air grows warmer and the leaves reach their full size. It's one of the most delightful sights of the west-coast rainforest.

To the indigenous people who settled southwestern

British Columbia thousands of years ago, the Big Leaf maple, like most flora, was an important resource. Known as the 'paddle tree' by tribes that used its relatively hard wood to make canoe paddles, it was also used for dishes, spoons, rattles, pipes, adze handles and clothing hooks, with the inner bark devoted to baskets, rope and whisks. The sap was used by interior peoples for making maple syrup, an enterprise that has been taken up recently on Vancouver Island by hobbyists, community groups, and even a few business people who have discovered that despite a low sugar content and slow-flowing sap, Acer macrophyllum produces a flavourful syrup that has found a niche market and even inspired an annual Big Leaf maple syrup festival in Duncan, adding one more component to the local food scene.

Furniture-makers and luthiers are the other primary seekers of Big Leaf maple, discounting the owners of fireplaces and wood stoves who value its slow-burning qualities. Highly figured and hard, Big Leaf maple produces beautiful furniture and gorgeous stringed instrument backs and sides, which led Robert to suggest it for the back and sides of my guitar.

We'd been looking online and calling around to tonewood suppliers on the Island and mainland and even into Alberta and Washington State. Although we'd found a couple of good possibilities, the price for a suitable pair of Big Leaf maple billets was high – three hundred and fifty dollars or more for master grade.

Robert preferred to select the pieces in person rather than having them shipped from afar. I too was in favour of a local supplier and so we decided to keep our eyes open and Robert said he'd contact Jim Ham to see if he had any sources.

A few weeks into our search Robert emailed to say that Ham, who was looking for more maple himself, had proposed a trip to Nanaimo and Ladysmith, mid-Island communities two hours from Victoria. I was invited to join them, but a late winter cold sidelined me, and so one Saturday morning Robert joined Ham and two other luthiers, Ted White from nearby Metchosin and Mark Hollinger, a violin maker visiting from Missoula, Montana, on a maple-seeking mission. Robert promised me a detailed report when he returned.

Sunday came and went with no word. Finally on Monday Robert sent a short email announcing success. A few days later, visiting his workshop to view the wood, I encountered an animated luthier with a good story to tell.

"Well, it starts with the name of the place," said Robert, laughing as he revealed that "Gorgeous Boards" (presumably a play on the wrestler Gorgeous George) had provided the maple for my guitar. Located in an industrial area of Nanaimo, it was a one-man custom sawmill that, like others on the Island, had sprung up in the wake of the wholesale decline of the west-coast forest industry. A few decades ago major sawmills dotted the Island, but with their demise, smaller operators cultivated niche markets supplying specialty woods to furniture builders, instrument makers and the like.

When Starr showed them around, they uncovered, in a forgotten corner, an entire pallet of quarter-sawn double bass, cello, violin, and guitar backs and sides that had been air drying for six years. The find of a decade for a quartet of luthiers looking for well-aged wood!

The story got better as he recounted how Hollinger, whom he described as "brilliant" at reading the figure of wood through saw cuts that would hide the quality from less perceptive eyes, tore the pallet apart and quickly graded each piece by holding it up to the light and assessing its figure. In a whirlwind of activity he set aside the pieces he wanted, sparking a competition amongst the other luthiers to begin identifying specific chunks they wanted for their individual projects. Jim Ham stopped the feeding frenzy by pulling them aside and saying, "Look, why don't we offer to buy the whole pallet and split it up later. We'll get a much better price."

A few minutes and several thousand dollars later, the deal was completed and four happy luthiers strode out of Gorgeous Boards, the owners of not one, but two pallets of instrument-quality Big Leaf maple, having discovered a second pallet piled high with random chunks that Starr was only too happy to part with at a bargain basement price.

Robert and I turned to examining the bookmatched billets he'd secured for my guitar. Unlike the rough-hewn chunk we began with for the top, these boards, uniformly quarter-sawn and roughly two feet long, nine inches wide and about an inch thick, would need much less work to prepare for glueing and carving.

I attempted, like Hollinger, to read the grain through the saw cuts but it was only when Robert squared and smoothed the pieces on his thickness sander that my untrained eyes could even see it. Even then it was faint, but the distinctive tiger-stripe pattern jumped out when he flipped the boards around and oriented them with the angled stripes lining up in the middle where the two edges would join. I imagined that this pattern – or figure as it's technically called – would really leap out when Robert applied the finish.

Pleased at what he'd found, I left Robert to glue the billets together, knowing that he'd follow the same steps he'd used for the top. Once the two boards were one, he'd use the mould to trace the shape of the body before cutting it out with the bandsaw. There was no need for me to see that again. I could wait until he was ready to start carving.

I next saw Robert on a bright, blustery spring day ankle deep in wood shavings in the backyard by his workshop. He had the maple back secured on a Workmate and was carving with controlled abandon with a new tool he'd acquired from Lee Valley, a supplier of specialty woodworking tools. Called a 'freestyle woodcarver,' the small circular blade with its hardened teeth and clear plastic guard that attached to an angle grinder behaved like the tip of a chainsaw, allowing Robert to make plunge and lateral cuts that removed a lot of wood at once.

Wearing his yellow ear protectors and a white dust mask, he was hunched over when I arrived, sweeping the roaring grinder back and forth in short strokes, rapidly hollowing out the inside of the guitar back.

Shavings sprayed like snow, covering his legs and falling to the ground. He saw me, stopped the machine, brushed his legs clean, and in the silence that ensued told me the new tool was working well, explaining that he'd practiced on a rough piece of maple to get a feel first and to ensure that on the real thing he wouldn't go too far. He said the tool was saving him a lot of time, particularly in working with the maple, a much harder and more difficult-to-carve wood than the Sitka spruce. Indeed, in less than an hour the work was finished and the back was ready for fine carving by hand. We were making great leaps forward.

Sixteen

EIGENFREQUENCIES

The days lengthened and warmed as Robert continued his work on the back. One late spring day I arrived at his workshop to find most of the carving completed except for the fine-tuning that would come when he assembled the body. The back, with its beautiful tiger-striped figure, lay on his desk illuminated by window-light. I admired it for a moment, running my fingers over the smooth surface. Then Robert said, "Pick it up and feel the weight."

It was like the difference between a loaf of white bread and a dense rye. The top had felt light and airy but the back was heavy and substantial. I wondered how the weight would affect the sound because I knew the goal was to produce as light an instrument as possible. Robert was also surprised but seemed unconcerned.

A cubic-foot block of Big Leaf maple, at twenty-percent moisture content, weighs about thirty-four pounds, whereas Sitka spruce is only twenty-eight pounds. Western red cedar, another tonewood used in guitar building, is lighter still at twenty-three pounds per cubic foot. Balsa – not typically used in instrument building although some luthiers have experimented with it – is the lightest of all at eleven pounds. At the other end of the spectrum, a cubic-foot block of teak weights forty-five pounds and lignum vitae or ironwood, the hardest and densest of all woods, a whopping eighty-six pounds.

Weight is determined by density, which in turn is determined by the cellular structure, the component materials and the amount of air present in the wood. Balsa is seventy percent air and hence perfect for building the model airplanes I tossed around as a kid. Lignum vitae is so dense and devoid of air it sinks in water and can even be used to make bearings for machines, including for the first nuclear-powered submarine, the USS Nautilus. It was used by the San Francisco railway system to make insulators for the overhead cables that powered the trolleys. Many of these wooden insulators survived the fires of the 1906 earthquake that burned hot enough to soften iron poles and melt copper wire. Some of the original insulators remained in service for over a hundred years, being replaced only when other components had to be renewed. Perhaps folksinger Pete Seeger was thinking of such longevity when he carved the neck of his banjo out of lignum vitae in 1955.

Sitka spruce and similar softwoods have long been valued for their desirable weight-to-strength ratio – so desirable, in fact, that they were used in airplane construction, starting before World War I. Howard Hughes' infamous 'Spruce Goose,' the massive World War II cargo plane built in response to a metal shortage and the need to move troops and cargo during the war, was constructed of wood – laminated birch, it turns out, despite its name. Five stories high with the wingspan the length of a football field, it remains the largest plane ever built. Because it was completed after the war ended, it flew only once on a one-mile test flight seventy feet above the water off a California beach in 1947. Hughes employed a crew to maintain it in a climate-controlled hangar until his death in 1976. It currently resides at a museum in Oregon.

Weight-to-strength ratio is also important when building a guitar. Spruce and cedar are good choices for the top because they are light and strong and transmit sound well. When carved or sanded within certain tolerances they transmit the vibrations of the strings efficiently, while still having the strength to avoid cracking under a hundred pounds or more of string tension.

They also vibrate more easily than hardwoods and at a lower frequency, thus producing a warm, rich sound. For this reason spruce is favoured not only for guitars, but also violins, violas, cellos and double basses.

Maple has long been the number one choice for the back and sides of a violin and consequently an archtop guitar because of its acoustical properties and its pleasing figure, which adds to the aesthetic quality of the instrument. According to Bob Benedetto, a hard maple such as Acer saccharum – the rock or sugar maple found in eastern North America – will create a bright sound, whereas a softer maple like Acer pseudoplantanus – the European sycamore maple – will be more mellow.

Big leaf is a soft maple, although 'soft' is a relative term since all maple is dense and hard when compared to spruce and cedar. These qualities make it ideal for the back and sides because it reflects sound well and adds brightness to the mix. The brightness creates more definition and projection in the notes, avoiding any tendency towards muddiness that might occur if only softwoods were employed.

Early luthiers discovered the acoustical properties of various woods through trial and error. Many of their findings have since been validated by scientific inquiry that has examined the acoustical performance of different species, looking at factors such as how fast and efficiently sound travels through the material and how well it radiates sound waves that reach the listener's ear.

The analysis of sound has extended to the frequencies generated when a string sounds. When I pluck the A-string on my guitar, I hear a single tone but it's actually made up of multiple frequencies. The lowest or fundamental frequency dominates and determines the pitch, but complementary harmonic overtones mix with the fundamental tone to create the sound I hear. Also called 'eigenfrequencies,' these overtones or upper partials occur at defined mathematical intervals. If the fundamental tone is vibrating at 440 cycles per second (Hz), then the first harmonic overtone will be 880 Hz, the second 1320 Hz, the third 1760 Hz, and so on.

The relative loudness of each overtone determines the tonal quality or timbre of the instrument. Daniel J. Levitin in his book *This Is Your Brain on Music* notes that a saxophone sounds like a saxophone because of its particular tonal fingerprint. When I sound that A-string on my guitar so my friend Ron can tune his tenor sax to it, we both end up playing the same note with the same frequency but no one would ever mistake his sax for my guitar because each instrument has a different loudness profile in its mix of frequencies.

Levitin notes that all things in the universe have sonic profiles that determine their timbre or tonal character. Kick your garbage can and it will sound different from your garage door. Tap two different glasses in your kitchen and you'll get two different sounds. Blow on two different sized pop bottles and the tones will vary. These differences occur because of the characteristic structure of the objects and the nature of the materials of which they are made. When you kick that door, tap that glass, or blow into that bottle, you are exciting the molecules in the materials. The oscillations of the molecules send out certain frequencies that cause the air molecules to vibrate. Our ears pick up the oscillations, and through some miracle of physiology, detect the tonal character of the object. We can do it for human voices, the sounds of the forest, or a musical instrument.

Timbre or tonal character is also determined by overtones that are not exact multiples of the fundamental tone. These 'inharmonic partials,' as they are called, will be slightly out of pitch and will add their own colour or texture, further defining the quality of the instrument.

Not all instruments display such inharmonicity, but guitars and pianos do because tensioned strings can be affected by wear, dirt, a misaligned part or variability in their construction. This inharmonicity gives an acoustic piano or guitar much of its character. Early builders of synthesized electronic pianos discovered that they couldn't simply reproduce a characteristic set of harmonic overtones with a particular loudness profile to imitate the sound of an acoustic piano. If they did, it sounded artificial. They had to introduce inharmonic partials to make an electronic instrument sound more authentic.

Linda Ronstadt tells an interesting story in her memoir *Simple Dreams* that illustrates this principle. She had Brian Wilson sing and record harmony parts for "Adios," a Jimmy Webb ballad released on her *Cry Like a Rainstorm* album. Wilson recorded five tracks for each part, fifteen tracks in all. Ronstadt noticed he wasn't concerned that a few of the tracks were slightly out of tune when he recorded them. Later when he mixed the tracks, he took advantage of the 'chorus' effect created by the slightly out-of-pitch tracks to produce what Ronstadt calls "the creamy vocal smoothness instantly recognizable as the Beach Boys." A hint of inharmonicity was an important part of their sound and gave it much of its character. Wilson was using a technique he picked up from The Four Freshmen whereby he intentionally sang slightly off-pitch to incorporate inharmonic overtones into the sound.

Before Bach came along, the western scale contained twenty notes. Between F and G, for example, there was F-sharp, G-double-flat and G-flat. Bach reduced the scale to twelve tones to simplify it, in the process removing quarter tones that added richness. The Four Freshmen, the Beach Boys, and other choral singers still hit those quarter tones as they blend their voices, creating a richly layered effect, not always attainable on modern instruments.

Acoustic pianos take advantage of this phenomenon. Open the top of a piano and you'll notice that except for the lowest bass notes, the hammers strike two or even three strings for a given note. Piano tuners don't tune the strings assigned to a particular piano key identically. They tune them slightly out of pitch with each other to create a blended tone that is rich and balanced in character.

Pat Metheny told me that one of the reasons Linda Manzer's guitars stand out to him is that he hears so much more "information" in the notes when he plays one of her guitars. Presumably he's hearing the ability of the instrument to produce a particularly rich tonal profile through the combination of carefully selected tonewoods and Manzer's skill as a builder.

He also remarked on the evenness of the tones from top to bottom. Most guitarists will attest that guitars don't always display such consistency. The midrange notes may sound good but the bass tones will be boomy. Or the bass will sound good but the treble will be thin. Metheny noticed the richness and balance the very first time he played a Manzer guitar.

If you sound the A-string on five different acoustic guitars, you'll hear differences in tonal character. The contrast won't be as dramatic as between a sax and a guitar but it will be there. On one guitar the note may ring quite bright while on another it may be darker. On one it may sustain longer. On another it may sound richer. The type of guitar, the materials used to build it, and the quality of its construction are the factors that determine the differences. A big dreadnought has a different sound than a small-bodied parlour guitar. A guitar built of spruce and maple sounds quite different from one built of cedar and mahogany. And of course a steel string instrument has a different sound than one that uses nylon strings.

One thing was clear to me as I contemplated the carved back I held in my hands – no single factor would determine the sound of my finished guitar. The woods we used, the shape they took and Robert's skill would create an instrument like no other. How it would sound and what tonal fingerprint would emerge was still a mystery, but with the top and back carved, I could let out a sigh of relief because we'd completed two major legs of our journey.

Seventeen

ART THAT SINGS

Robert surprised me one day by revealing that he'd applied for arts funding to travel in the summer to Cambridge, England, to study violin-making. The carving of the top and back had awakened in him an old desire to build a violin and bow. As well he wanted to learn more about the finer aspects of carving a soundboard to be sure he did the best possible job on my guitar. The Benedetto book and his own experience had taken him quite far, but he was feeling less confident about the fine tuning of the top and back that would come just before he assembled the body. As he would admit later in a presentation he gave to a group of woodworkers: "I really didn't know what I was doing when it came to judging the final thickness [of the top and back]."

Applying for arts funding is a challenge at the best of times, but for a luthier a critical question comes to mind. At least it came to my mind. Is guitar-making an art form like sculpting, drawing or painting? Would an arts council that typically funds visual, written, musical and movement arts give a grant to a guitar maker?

We seldom think about what art is unless we're challenged to do so by an audacious practitioner who mounts a toilet on a gallery wall, paints blue and red stripes on an eighteen-foot-high canvas, or exhibits a dead shark in a tank of formaldehyde. When such an event hits the news, predictable responses pinball through the media: "That's not art!" "Any idiot could do that!" "My two-year-old could do a better job!"

However reactionary these outbursts are, they highlight a question that most people consider when deciding whether something is a work of art: does it show refined skill? Has the artist spent hundreds or even thousands of hours learning and perfecting his craft?

Finely-made handcrafted guitars certainly fit this criterion. To produce an instrument that is light, balanced, responsive and aesthetically pleasing requires an uncommon degree of skill attained through hundreds of hours of work. I've seen a few first guitars produced by inexperienced builders. They might look and sound okay, but they usually lack a refinement found in the work of experienced luthiers. They are like the early work of a painter who goes on to transcend craft and become a luminous artist. Set beside later works, first efforts often shrink in stature.

But the demonstration of skill alone isn't enough to define something as a work of art. A pilot can demonstrate great skill landing a plane in inclement weather, a hockey player deftly stick-handling a puck down the ice through a series of defenders, or a juggler keeping five flaming torches in the air on a windy day, but these demonstrations of ability don't constitute art. To call something art we want more. We seek an experience that transcends the work itself.

I remember reading John Keats in high school. His "Beauty is truth, truth beauty," line in *Ode on a Grecian Urn* triggered my first thoughts about the role of art in the world and its ability to express something beyond itself. Before reading that poem, if I looked at a painting or photograph, I might have thought it was 'beautiful' but I never understood the implications of my response. As vague as the word 'truth' was (and is), the poem helped me understand that an object had to offer something more than itself to be called a work of art.

Sometime later in university I bumped into Plato's theory of Forms, and while I didn't comprehend it fully, I did understand that he was speaking of ideal "blueprints" that resided not in the relative physical world but in what philosophers have sometimes called the transcendent. A well-crafted Grecian urn could be beautiful but could never fully embody "Beauty" because the urn was a physical object, a representation that had its limitations and imperfections and that would change and deteriorate with time. But it could trigger an aesthetic response and draw the viewer's mind closer to the abstract ideal, a lofty goal that Plato linked to the progress of the soul.

Immanuel Kant, an eighteenth-century philosopher, postulated a more modern notion of beauty that influences our view of art today. Cynthia Freeland, in her book *But Is It Art: An Introduction to Art Theory* notes that Kant felt that beauty could be found, not in some abstract ideal, but in the concrete reality of the work itself. Just as the colours, textures and form of a rose trigger a mental and emotional response that causes us to label it 'beautiful,' the physical attributes of an artwork can elicit an aesthetic response in which we acknowledge the transcendent beauty of a human creator's work.

Kant said this response must be independent of the function of the object. The function of a flower is to perpetuate the species, but that has nothing to do with our recognition of the flower's beauty. We could say that the function of a painting is to decorate a room but our apprehension of its inherent beauty transcends that role. Kant used the phrase "purposiveness without a purpose" to describe this phenomenon. As Freeland explains, we respond to the design of the object through our imagination and intellect regardless of its function or purpose.

According to Freeland, Kant's legacy carried on well into the twentieth century as new works from artists like Picasso, Cézanne, and Pollock challenged traditional views. Critics encouraged audiences to appreciate these works for their aesthetic qualities, not their subject matter or verisimilitude. These commentators generally viewed art as existing outside of life and politics. Freeland notes that one English critic, Clive Bell (1881-1964), used the metaphor of "cold white peaks" to emphasize art's distance from everyday life. In this view, encounters with art are experiences with form, not content. Those interactions take place in a pure and distant Shangri-La of the mind well away from the dust and bustle of everyday life.

Whatever their origins and permeations, these notions make clear that, at the very least, an object must go beyond mere function to be considered art. To be art, an archtop guitar must do more than be well-made and create pleasing sound under the fingers of a musician. Hanging on the wall or sitting on its stand, it should trigger an aesthetic response even before it's played.

John Monteleone, a New York luthier many consider the heir to John D'Angelico and Jimmy D'Aquisto when it comes to New-York-built archtop guitars, was interviewed by the Metropolitan Museum of Art for their *Guitar Heroes* show in 2011, an exhibition that celebrated guitar makers from Renaissance Italy to contemporary New York. One of three American builders featured in the show (D'Angelico and D'Aquisto were the other two), Monteleone talked about the archtop guitar as an art object by comparing it to a painting where the eye is drawn to a particular area but has the freedom to move within the painting and return to the area of focus at will. "I like the guitar – if you are able to just look at it and not play it – to vibrate.

That to me is an instrument that is already in motion without even touching it."

Already in motion without even touching it. A guitar is obviously all about motion when played. One hand moves up and down the neck seeking new positions on the fingerboard while the fingers depress the strings in different combinations to form chords or play single-note lines. The other hand sets the strings in motion with fingertips, a pick or a thumb, sending the vibrating energy through the bridge to the top. The vibrating top causes the whole soundbox and the air within it to move, exciting molecules in the air, and sending waves of sound to the ears of the player and the listener.

Already in motion without even touching it? That's a completely different idea that invites us to see the guitar as a painting or sculpture.

Monteleone took his thinking one step further by noting that the guitar is unique among objects of art because it's both visual and auditory. "And now you walk up and play this instrument and it gives you this other dimension… that's what makes it as an art object really unique because it behaves like no other art object there is. It's not like a painting, it's not like a sculpture, a statue, or a piece of jewelry. In that sense…a guitar is multi-dimensional."

In a followup email interview with me Monteleone explained his thinking further, noting that he'd seen "too many intruments that have a clinically stale appearance to them," and adding that a guitar maker becomes an artist "when the instrument speaks so well for itself" that people "will want to know who made it" and how they can have one. He also made it clear that "the bottom line and real substance of a musical instrument" is "how beautifully it sounds and plays."

Julian Lage is an internationally acclaimed American virtuoso guitarist who has been in the public eye ever since he performed as a child prodigy on stage with Carlos Santana at age eight and was the subject of the Mark Becker award-winning documentary *Jules at Eight*. He appreciates the visual art of the guitar, particularly the archtop.

Now in his late twenties, Lage shared his thoughts with me in a telephone interview from his home in New York.

"The archtop world to me is always kind of fascinating because in a lot of ways it's as aesthetically driven as the solid body world is. People take a lot of risks, do a lot of fancy colors, different shaped f-holes, different shaped headstocks – when done right it's really a work of art."

Lage was noting that the advent of the solid-body electric guitar allowed builders to experiment with visual design, a process that continues to this day. A flat-top guitar needs a soundbox of certain dimensions and characteristics to amplify the sound acoustically. A solid-body electric doesn't have these requirements because the vibrations are transmitted by a pickup directly to an amplifier. The body can be any shape or size imaginable, with the result that electric guitar builders have created everything from Gibson's futuristic 'Flying V' guitar of the fifties to Prince's curvy and sexually charged 'Cloud' guitar of the eighties. They've shaped the bodies into Ak-47 machine guns, skeletons, and tongues of flame, using everything from psychedelic paint jobs to fur and shattered glass to decorate them, taking the solid body electric guitar in radical and sometimes bizarre artistic directions.

Designers and builders of steel string flat-top guitars, in contrast, adhere to a relatively conservative aesthetic established in the nineteenth century when the guitar first became popular in North America. They incorporate decorative features, from abalone binding to spalted maple sound-hole rosettes, but the selection and finish of the tonewoods are the primary elements they manipulate for visual effect.

But even that is limited by concerns about sound. Backs and sides of most flat top guitars tend to be mahogany or rosewood, the tops spruce or sometimes cedar and the fingerboards ebony or rosewood. Body size and shape tend to follow the standards set by the C.F. Martin Company in its early designs. Large-bodied dreadnoughts, introduced by Martin in 1916, account for most steel string acoustic guitar sales. Smaller bodied guitars like the OM make up most of the remaining sales, with specialty guitars like parlour and folk guitars accounting for the rest. The nylon string classical world is even more aesthetically conservative.

This is not to say that acoustic flat-top builders haven't

created unique instruments. They have, one of the most interesting being the "Six String Nation" guitar built by Canadian luthier George Rizsanyi at the instigation of writer and broadcaster Jowi Taylor. Taylor conceived of the guitar in response to a perennial Canadian political issue that heated up in 1996 when the Parti Quebecois launched a referendum calling on Quebec to separate from Canada.

Built to encourage Canadian unity and find new symbols for the country – Taylor thought the old ones like the maple leaf and beaver had become tired and meaningless – the guitar incorporates sixty-three iconic elements representing Canadian history and culture in its construction, including wood from sources like the Bluenose II, Wayne Gretzky's hockey stick, and Pierre Trudeau's canoe paddle. Taylor also collected, among other things, gold from Maurice "Rocket" Richard's Stanley Cup rings, mastadon ivory from the Yukon and walrus tusk from Rankin Inlet. The project took years to complete and the guitar, dubbed "The Voyageur," has travelled across the country and has been played by a number of music icons, including Bruce Cockburn and Gordon Lightfoot. It's as much a political and cultural statement as a musical instrument.

Another Canadian luthier, William "Grit" Laskin, uses his flat-top guitars as "canvases" upon which he creates elaborate engraved inlay art he custom designs for his clients. Laskin goes well beyond mere decoration with one-of-a-kind designs that often cover the entire headstock and fingerboard. One such flat-top steel string, 'JATP49,' was conceived as a tribute to jazz pianist Oscar Peterson. The headstock displays a portrait of Peterson while the fingerboard sports a piano keyboard with hands playing it. ("JATP49" refers to Jazz at the Philharmonic, 1949, the New York concert at which Peterson, who was from Montreal, made his international debut.) Another guitar, called 'Imagine,' incorporates a portrait of John Lennon with four Lennon-related images portrayed within the letters of the song.

Four of Laskin's guitars are in the permanent collection of the Museum of Civilization, Canada's equivalent to the Smithsonian, and he's internationally recognized as a bold innovator in the flat-top world. Monteleone calls Laskin's work "stunning," and says, "his eyes are as good as his hands and his themes are always fascinating."

If the traditional jazz archtop has a dominant sensibility or aesthetic, it's Art Deco, the visual style that emerged in France after World War One and influenced the design of everything from skyscrapers and theatres to automobiles and refrigerators until its popularity faded during the Second World War.

An international, mass-produced phenomenon that was revived in the sixties and influences design even today, Art Deco married art with industry, using steel, concrete, aluminum, glass, and new materials like chrome and bakelite to create designs that announced, with considerable flourish, the optimism of the post-war years.

Unlike Art Nouveau, an earlier trend that favoured the organic and the curved, Art Deco preferred the manufactured and the straight, using repeating geometrical shapes and motifs, with strong lines and vibrant colours, to trumpet the power of technological progress. Stepped Art Deco skyscrapers reached for the sky while streamlined Art Deco automobiles powered down the highways and gleaming Art Deco radios blared the tunes of the Jazz Age.

The rise of Art Deco coincided with the emergence of the dance bands, and so it's not surprising that the archtop guitar should feature Art Deco designs, particularly since its most influential builders – D'Angelico and D'Aquisto – called New York home. New York is the most Art Deco and jazz-rich of all the great cities and these guitar makers only had to look to the facades and spires of the buildings around them – or to the elaborate lamps, clocks, radios, tables, chairs, and other consumer products that filled the display windows – for inspiration.

The Art Deco influence on a given archtop might extend to stair-stepped tuning pegs, a stepped tortoise-shell pickguard and an angled chrome tailpiece, but builders could go all out, too, using rare woods and expensive inlays, creating a product that was as much artistic statement as musical instrument. The results were stunningly beautiful but they could also be over-the-top with their extravagant display of ornamentation.

When D'Angelico passed his craft and artistic vision on to D'Aquisto, the tradition continued and blossomed as emerging archtop builders, unrestrained by expectation, experimented freely, although it's interesting to note that, according to Linda Manzer, Jimmy D'Aquisto didn't fully realize his own creative vision. In *Blue Guitar* she reports him saying to her, "You are so lucky. You can do anything you want; everyone expects me to build what I always build." She adds that he felt constrained by traditional archtop design in his early years and only later in life began to experiment with guitars like the Classic, the Solo, the Centura, the Avant Garde, and the Advance. She believes these guitars only hint at what he could have done had he lived longer.

While not every handmade guitar "vibrates" in the way that Monteleone suggests, many do qualify as objects of art because they are finely crafted and they inspire an aesthetic response independent of their musical function. Like its electric cousin and some flat-tops, the archtop has become an open canvas upon which a guitar maker can paint a complete artistic story.

The Blue Guitar project alone shows the range and depth of this blossoming. Flip through Vose's book and you'll see everything from D'Angelico's stunning Teardrop New Yorker with its radically curved and stepped design elements to Jim Triggs's "more is more" take-off on the New Yorker with its abalone binding and pickguard, highly engraved tailpiece, and sunburst fingerboard. These guitars and others like them are beautiful objects that make bold statements, inspiring awe and discussion.

In his preface to *Blue Guitar*, Gary Sturm of the Smithsonian makes the case for the guitars in the collection transcending their function and becoming art objects.

"The Blue Guitars of the Chinery Collection are a tribute to all contemporary musical instrument makers. They are a reminder that old-world traditions continue to be expressed through individual craftsmanship and that the art of lutherie is thriving in our contemporary society. But because they are a tribute to the state of guitar making and a link in the chain of craft tradition, they are more than just guitars. Blue guitars become sculpture. They break through traditional barriers and, perceived as artworks, open doorways to surreal imagination."

Eighteen

JULIAN LAGE

With the back and top carved and the f-holes cut, Robert was ready to make the sides. He'd already cut two strips of Big Leaf maple about three inches wide, an eighth-of-an-inch thick and thirty inches long. His task now was to bend them to conform to the mould he'd built earlier and that to this point had been used only as a template. Now it would take on its most important function – housing the body as it was shaped and assembled.

Early luthiers employed a metal pipe sitting atop a bed of hot coals to bend wood. Linda Manzer had shown me her own homemade bending iron that was nothing more than a piece of pipe acquired from a plumber that she'd attached to a heat gun, a simple device that wasn't that far removed from the method Stradivari must have used to bend the sides of his violins.

Robert preferred a commercially made bending iron that was thermostatically controlled and offered two different radii on a tear-drop-shaped cast aluminum post, allowing for varied bends and precise temperature selections for different kinds of wood. He explained that

144

this gave him much greater control over the process and that it was much easier for him to make the micro-adjustments needed to ensure a precise fit.

First he spritzed the maple strip with an ammonia solution to soften the wood cells to facilitate bending. After that he held the strip with both hands against the wider side of the heated metal teardrop post, applying pressure and rocking the strip gently back and forth until the fibres started to give and the wood began to relax. As he proceeded he repeatedly checked the curve he was creating against the interior curve of the mould, returning the wood to the iron numerous times to achieve the desired shape.

He explained that wood fibres don't stretch. Under heat and pressure they collapse and crinkle, and so it was important that he take care to avoid cracking or tearing the wood, particularly on tight bends.

Watching Robert work, I once again admired his quiet patience, thinking that I'd be hurried and anxious in this situation. Robert felt his way with his fingers as he coaxed the wood to take a new shape. It was less an act of will than an act of faith – faith borne of much experience and more than a little technical understanding of the way that wood cells and fibres behave under heat and pressure.

I couldn't help but think that his hands and fingers were joining a long line of hands and fingers bending wood over time for various purposes – the shepherd's crook used to snare the leg of a sheep, the cedar ribs that lined the birch bark canoes of Canada's indigenous people, the wooden rim of the wheel that circled through dust, dirt and mud on a nineteenth century pony cart and the arc of a form used to shape the curves in the concrete sidewalk at the corner of my street.

Robert went back and forth numerous times to get the first strip to fit. Finally satisfied, he clamped it in place inside the mould and began work on the strip that would form the other side.

With both in place, he then turned to the neck block and tail block, rectangular chunks of wood fitted inside the guitar at either end of the body to add strength and provide gluing surfaces for the top, back and sides. The neck block would also provide an attachment point for the heel of the neck.

He showed me how the sides would be butt jointed where they met at either end, and the blocks would be glued atop each joint and held temporarily in place with an internal clamping system that pushed the whole structure against the inside of the mould.

One clamp consisted of two blocks of wood joined by an adjustable turnbuckle that fit across the narrow internal waist of the guitar body. The other employed two circular pieces joined with a flexible stick spanning the distance lengthwise and applying pressure longitudinally between the neckblock and tailblock. Like so many of his self-crafted devices, the two clamps provided a simple, ingenious, low-cost method for accomplishing a specific task.

After months of work, the body of my guitar was finally taking shape. Soon the sides would be in place and then the top and back would be added. After weeks of slow carving we were making rapid progress. The end of the first major phase, the building of the body, was in sight.

A discussion of archtop guitars inevitably must lead to the players who play them. The good fortune of the CBC contract had already introduced me to one – Pat Metheny – who spent years playing a Gibson ES-175, the quintessential electric jazz archtop. But there were other players I wanted to talk with to get a fuller understanding of the archtop from a musician's perspective.

As already mentioned in the previous chapter, Julian Lage was one of them. The youngest musician I would interview (he was twenty-six when we spoke in 2014), he had started playing when he was only five. He first appeared on record at age eleven with David Grisman and at age twelve played the 2000 Grammy Awards. Watching that Grammy show was jazz great Gary Burton who sent the young Lage a letter inviting him to play with him at an upcoming gig in Monterey, California, near Lage's family home.

The gig went well and Lage played with Burton periodically for the next few years. Like Pat Metheny before him, he was eventually invited to join Burton's band, a right of passage for some of the best jazz guitarists in the world.

I met Lage following a duo concert he played with Nels Cline in Victoria, and we agreed to talk by phone when he returned to his home in New York City a few weeks later.

As well as sharing his thoughts on the general aesthetic values of archtop guitars (discussed in the previous chapter), he explained how he'd come to own and play one.

He'd started on a Fender Stratocaster solid-body because he played blues when he was very young. He said he was also something of a "flat-top guitar nerd" growing up. But he soon became interested in archtops.

"Jazz greats always seemed to have them, and so I was drawn to them because they were using them. I thought there must be something to them. It's only when I got an archtop that I realized what I liked about it and started adapting my playing to incorporate its attributes."

The attributes he noticed on his first archtop, a Gibson ES-175, were a warm tone and a more percussive attack, qualities more suited to jazz than the long, singing notes available on his Stratocaster, which, as we know from Eric Clapton's example, is a great blues guitar but is not as commonly seen in the hands of a jazz musician, although jazz greats from Ed Bickert to Bill Frisell have played solid bodies, usually Telecasters, with great success.

Lage acquired a Linda Manzer 'Blue Note' archtop he first saw at the Healdsburg Guitar Festival in California when he was only eleven.

"That guitar – something seemed different about it. It was the whole experience that swept me up too. I was seeing the most magnificent guitar I'd ever seen. It has this quality about it where you say, 'wow that's a beautiful instrument.' It's gorgeous to look at, it feels great, it sounds great, but the other part of it which is equal to that, is that it's made by Linda. Linda as a person is so warm and just kind of enchanting. For me, even as a little boy, I thought, 'wow that's a beautiful person.' She's funny and whimsical, extremely hard working, takes a lot of risks, very courageous, and a true artist. The combination of the two, of seeing it in guitar form and seeing her as a human – I didn't need convincing – I was just kind of speechless. I'd never had this kind of relationship to a guitar and this was before I even owned it."

Manzer had built the guitar for a Canadian player, but when she returned to Toronto, the sale fell through. Lage happened to email her to inquire about her waiting list (which was four years long) and learned that the guitar he'd seen in Healdsburg was now available. She said she'd be happy to send it to him if he wanted to give it a try. Once he got it in his hands, there was no letting go and so Manzer worked out an arrangement whereby he could buy it.

"I've grown up with that guitar. Everything I've learned, I've learned pretty much on that guitar. That's home base for me," Lage said with sincere affection and enthusiasm for an instrument that clearly means a lot to him.

Unlike the guitar Robert was building for me, Lage's guitar has a five-ply maple and mahogany laminate top and back with solid maple sides, a configuration that Lage says makes it nuanced and clear but also stable and predictable. It doesn't change in different climates. He can travel from gig to gig, pull it out of its case and it will always be in tune and performance-ready unlike solid-topped guitars that can be susceptible to climatic changes.

Jim Hall, a man Metheny calls the father of the modern jazz guitar and one of the most respected and influential jazz players in history, long argued that laminated wood was a better material for the top of an electric archtop because much of the tone is produced by the amplifier. As well, such a guitar is less susceptible to feedback, often the bane of any guitarist who plays an amplified hollow-body.

Lage also liked his Blue Note because it didn't have a prominent arch – which made it closer to a flat-top in construction – but unlike many flat-tops, it didn't over-accentuate certain frequencies. "It's not a melodramatic guitar," was the way he put it, comparing it to a Loar L-5 from the nineteen twenties he'd played in Toronto that was "the most responsive, beautiful instrument I've ever played." He noted that like the Manzer, the Loar was practically a flat-top with f-holes. "I've played a lot of archtops. I tend to lean towards ones that have very little actual arch."

He also appreciated the aesthetics of the Manzer guitar, noting that while it was fairly traditional, it had a few interesting features like a stylized hole in the headstock, which made it distinctive but didn't overwhelm with a lot of fancy inlay – "more conceptual than decorative" was how he put it. "I think she's struck a perfect balance with it – it's just a fantastic guitar."

I asked Lage about Jimmy D'Aquisto's assertion that in many ways the archtop was a perfect guitar because it was versatile enough to suit almost any player in any style. Lage considered this at length, noting that a lot depended on the playing context.

"Archtops don't have spillover into frequencies that you don't want. With a rosewood dreadnought, for example, you can get a thing where the bass is overwhelming and the high end is kind of thin, or with a small bodied flat-top, depending on how it's braced, you could have something that's really sweet or that's honky where all you hear is the G and the B string and there's no low E. So from a frequency-spectrum-point-of-view the archtop is pretty ideal."

"Having said that, the difficulty is that perfection isn't necessarily what fits with other instruments that well. Everything is even and clear but sometimes I've noticed that when I'm playing an archtop with other instruments, everything sounds punctuated when you wish it could slip into the fold a little more. I felt that with the L-5 (a Gibson L-5 he owns but doesn't play much now) I loved it but I could only exist in front of the other frequencies. If you listen to Eddie Lang and the other archtop innovators, you hear that there's a style built around being very forward and being undeniably there. My interest in archtop guitars has always been about context and how people incorporate them and use them."

To illustrate his point further he contrasted Maybelle Carter, whom he considered a more rhythm-oriented player on her L-5, with David Rawlings, whom he saw as almost mandolin-like with the soaring fills and solo lines he plays on his 1935 Epiphone Olympic archtop.

One final thing he said left me thinking: "I don't even think we know what an archtop guitar can do yet and that's exciting in a lot of ways."

He's fully aware that the archtop is still a relatively new instrument in the history of the guitar, and having undergone a revival with the advent modern lutherie, it's still finding its way in the guitar world outside of jazz.

I was taken by Lage's warmth, enthusiasm and thoughtful commentary. The archtop is in good hands with players like him around to appreciate it.

Nineteen

FRANK VIGNOLA/BUCKY PIZZARELLI

The next archtop guitarist I contacted was Frank Vignola, a New York player the great Les Paul put on his 'five most admired guitarists' list for the *Wall Street Journal.* Vignola has worked with the likes of Ringo Starr and Madonna, but jazz, particularly gypsy jazz, is his mainstay.

By any standard he's one of the most accomplished, versatile and captivating guitarists in the world with jaw-dropping technique and musicality. And he's spent a lot of time around archtop guitars.

Needless to say I was thrilled when he agreed to speak with me by telephone from North Carolina where he was with his son at a baseball camp. Already aware of the subject of our conversation from our email exchange, he wasted no time telling me about his personal history with the archtop.

"I grew up from the age of six playing on a 1958 D'Angelico New Yorker. An eighteen-inch. The guitar was bigger than me," said Vignola, explaining that it came to him via his step-grandmother who had married his grandfather after both were widowed. Her first husband had owned the D'Angelico along with a collection of 78s that featured the likes of Benny Goodman, Django Reinhardt and Johnny Smith, performers the young Vignola loved to listen to. "Between that and my father playing the Les Paul records…"

Vignola interrupted himself to note that Les Paul had started out playing acoustic archtop guitars and had created the solid-body electric by putting a railroad tie underneath an archtop so he could get more sustain and eliminate feedback.

"I was very friendly with Les and I would go over to his house many times late at night and he had that guitar still – the original Epiphone that he turned into a solid body."

A side note here: the original "log guitar," consisting of a four-by-four block of pine with a neck from a forties Gibson, a fingerboard from a Larsen guitar, and the sides from an Epiphone archtop, is now in the Country Music Hall of Fame in Nashville. As the story goes Paul tried playing the "log" on stage without the attached archtop sides but it wasn't well accepted visually and so he added them to make the guitar look more conventional.

Vignola expressed deep affection for the sound of the original archtops. "To me nothing beats those old archtops. There's just something about maybe the way they aged, the wood they used, the craftsmanship…those old Gibsons, those old Epiphones especially, no matter what model even if it's the cheaper Triumph model. They're so good…and as great as all the guitars are now like the Benedettos and the Thorells (Vignola now endorses a Thorell after endorsing Benedettos for years), I don't think you'll ever be able to recapture the sound of those original archtop guitars."

I asked him what he specifically liked about the sound. "The mid-range of the guitar – that's what I love...you play a chord on the third, fourth and fifth string and it sounds like an organ. That's the only way I can explain it. That's the way I've always thought about it. I played an Epiphone Emperor for many, many years until I got my Benedetto. That guitar was just awesome. No cutaway, but the sound of it – you couldn't beat it, especially for rhythm."

Vignola was less interested in aesthetic qualities, particularly on old instruments. "It means nothing... matter of fact a guy came over for a lesson a while ago and he had a really old case, and he pulls out a late thirties Gibson L5. The top was beat up and the neck was worn – which to me means the guitar was played and that's why it sounded so good. If it's played professionally, it's going to have dings, it's going to be worn on the neck. I think the worse thing you can do with an old archtop guitar is refinish it. Then the whole sound changes."

"Aesthetics to me really means nothing. I even think cracks sometimes help the sound of archtop guitars. For instance my Benedetto La Venezia. Beautiful archtop guitar but from day one it wasn't quite right. That's the only way I can put it. It sounded great but it just wasn't quite right."

He then explained that his young son accidentally put two big cracks in the top of the La Venezia (a model that now retails for $22,000 US). "I went 'oh man' but after I got them fixed up, the guitar was like a new guitar. It sounds better than it did when there wasn't a crack. Now, does it devalue it? Yeah, I guess it does, but you know I'm more interested in it for the sound."

"Even my Frank Vignola model Benedetto, which was the last one Bob built for me. I cracked the side of it. I thought I was going to start practising again, and I reached for a piece of music and hit the guitar on the corner of the desk – that'll teach me to start practicing again…anyway a big crack went along the side and I got that fixed up. The guitar's better than ever."

It was interesting to hear Vignola champion the sonic value of well-travelled and even damaged guitars because his comments were similar to Pat Metheny's about his well worn Linda 6.

Metheny had explained to me that whenever he got a new guitar from Linda Manzer he usually dropped it right away and put a big ding in it. He didn't think it was intentional but rather some kind of unconscious thing that happened.

Manzer told me that she'd actually stopped installing special inlays on the guitars she built for Metheny because he ignored them. She'd only started doing them again after his guitar technician protested because she really enjoyed that aspect of Manzer's work.

Metheny's and Vignolas's remarks recall Neil Young's

comments in the Jonathan Demme film *Heart of Gold*. On stage at the Ryman Auditorium in Nashville, Young declared his love for Willie Nelson's guitar 'Trigger,' a heavily damaged old Martin nylon string that Nelson has played for years. Young made his comments while introducing "This Old Guitar," a song he'd written in honour of a Hank Williams guitar he'd acquired some years before. He clearly loved the authenticity of old instruments, perhaps seeing them as vessels of wisdom that hold all the music and life experience of the players who have played them before. Something authentic in an age where authenticity is hard to find.

I asked Vignola why he played archtops. "I choose to play archtops because I just love the lead sound of them. I love the richness of the tone, especially archtops that are very even sounding, meaning that every note sounds the same from lowest to the highest."

"You know, I love the adjustable bridge, too, because guitars do fluctuate in their action depending on the weather and so it's nice to have the option to move the screws a little bit and have your action right. Also it's easy to adjust the intonation because the intonation is very tricky on guitars. And so you can move that bridge a little bit and boom, your guitar goes into perfect tune and you start to get all the overtones."

Vignola also appreciated the sonic character of a good flat-top and compared it to the sound of a piano. "When you hit that low open E string – that'll sound really big and full – that's what I miss on the archtops."

He noted that in his gypsy jazz duo, Vinny Raniolo intentionally plays a flat-top to create contrast with Vignola's archtop. "Having that difference of sound between the archtop and the flat-top really creates one very unique sound."

Vignola's comments called to mind something that Julian Lage had said about playing acoustic guitars in general. He loved playing them because there was a certain responsiveness with an acoustic instrument that he didn't get in an electric guitar, a certain quality of information that didn't come through an amplifier.

"There's the notes and there's the way you attack it," Lage had said. "But there's another indescribable thing. I would almost describe it as an afterglow. You play it and then you hear the sound tossing around in the body – like a shadow in a way. I especially notice it with my L-5 from the thirties. You play a note, there's the attack and then there's all these stages of decay – it's very stimulating."

Vignola concluded our conversation by giving me a remarkable gift – Bucky Pizzarelli's phone number. "You should talk to Bucky about archtops," he said. "He's got an incredible collection. Tell him Frank told you to call. He'll be happy to talk to you."

Bucky Pizzarelli is a jazz guitar legend who's played archtops for over seventy years. He started at the tail end of the big band era in the mid-forties with the Vaughan Monroe Orchestra and carried on through the decades as an in-demand studio and performing musician. He played rhythm guitar for Benny Goodman, Frank Sinatra, Stephane Grappelli and a host of other jazz greats. He recorded duo albums with the likes of Zoot Sims, Scott Hamilton, and Frank Vignola. Most recently he recorded with Diana Krall's band on Paul McCartney's Grammy-winning standards album *Kisses on the Bottom*. Widely considered one of the best jazz rhythm players in history, he's also a master of the solo seven-string electric archtop, a skill he learned from George Van Eps, the man who pioneered the seven-string archtop and the solo fingerstyle approach to it. And he's fathered two well-known jazz musicians – guitarist/vocalist John Pizzarelli and bassist Martin Pizzarelli.

Talking with Bucky was going to be like talking with jazz itself.

As it turned out, in this interview at least, he was a man of few words. Here's an edited version.

RG. What attracted you to the archtop?

BP. That's what you had to do in those days if you played in a band. You had to play an archtop. You couldn't play rhythm with the electric – that was a no-no.

RG. What do you love about archtops?

BP. In the right hands you can't beat that sound. It's a great, great sound - George Van Eps playing rhythm guitar – no matter what record, you can always tell it's him playing.

RG. Do you have a favourite guitar in your collection of archtops?

BP. There's an Epiphone I sort of like. I never use it

professionally. I did a few recordings but it's a beautiful guitar. It's got a good crack – you know what I mean? They made good guitars in those days."

At this point in the conversation I interrupted him to question the word 'crack,' thinking back to Frank Vignola's comments. But he didn't mean a literal crack – it was an expression he used to describe the quality of the sound.

RG. I understand you're an avid painter. How important are the aesthetic or decorative aspects of the archtop guitar to you?

BP. I don't care about that.

RG. How important was the archtop guitar in the development of jazz?

BP. When you heard the right guy playing a guitar like that there's no better sound in the world because that's the body of the whole record – that rhythm guitar – the after beat.

RG. You mean on recordings with guys like Frank Sinatra, Tony Bennett, etc.?

BP. That's right, that's what you hear.

RG. What do you feel as a player when you play?

BP. You can hear that after beat. When you do that after beat – the boom-chink, the boom-chink. There's nothing like it. You know it's happening.

RG. Do you feel one of those old guitars in your body? Does it really vibrate?

BP. Oh definitely. Exactly.

RG. Any archtops that got away from you, that you

wish you still had?

BP. No, not really. I knew which ones were great and I kept them.

Pizzarelli finished our chat with a story about an archtop that did get away but only for awhile.

"I just bought a D'Angelico for two hundred and fifty bucks and Les Paul happened to stop by the house, and I said, 'Les, try this out,' and he just strummed it once and said, 'Let me take this home for awhile.' I said, 'Sure!' I let him take it."

"He kept it for a whole year! I saw a picture in a local paper and it said, 'Les Paul playing his music at his house' and he was playing my guitar! He knew more about archtops than anybody I know."

My chat with Pizzarelli meant I'd talked with three generations of archtop players who all share a love for the instrument. And as it turned out, even the guy best known for the development of the solid-body guitar (Les Paul) was an archtop lover. It seemed that the archtop was in good hands and would be around for awhile.

Twenty

GO-BARS

With the approach of summer the construction of the guitar slowed and stopped. Robert had received his arts grant and was spending most of his time working on the violin top and back that he would take to his course in England. I began preparing for an August visit from my closest friend from Paris and an October trip with my wife to southeast Asia.

In July Robert emailed from Cambridge to say that the course was going well and that he'd met a great group of people. I didn't see him when he returned in August, but in September he and I travelled to Seattle to take in a Pat Metheny concert.

In late September just before my wife and I were scheduled to leave for Asia, Robert and I exchanged emails to discuss the resumption of the work. In his response to my query about when the project might be completed and what lay ahead, he wrote, "I can wait until you return to put the box [body] together and a February completion target seems reasonable, although you may find yourself in my workshop on a daily basis for awhile. After a final voicing of the top and back, I will be making and fitting the cross braces (takes a couple of hours); glueing kerfed linings on the sides (which takes an hour or so); then assembling the box (another hour or so, but fascinating). The next step is the bindings and purflings, which take a couple of days and involve a few steps. Plan on seeing me a lot in November."

November came and I arrived at Robert's shop to find that using the knowledge gleaned from his violin-building course, he'd already finished voicing the top

and back and was ready to attach the kerfed linings to the sides.

The linings were long, narrow triangular strips of wood slotted with vertical saw cuts every quarter inch or so to make them pliable so they could follow the interior curves of the sides without breaking. Once in place they would provide a glueing surface for the back and top because the guitar sides themselves were too thin to hold the body together.

Because Robert had already glued the sides, tail-block and neckblock together inside the mould in an earlier operation, attaching the kerfed linings was straightforward. He applied hide glue to the backs of the linings and fitted them inside the curving sides with their bases facing up and flush with the edges, creating a continuous glueing surface. To hold them in place while the glue set he used multi-coloured mini binder clips commonly found in stationary stores – yet another simple tool in his arsenal.

Before the body could be assembled, one more thing had to be done – Robert's custom-made label had to be glued to the inside of the back. The day we did this I felt we'd reached an important landmark in our guitar building journey. It was vaguely ceremonial when he placed the rectangular white label with its stylized Art Nouveau logo on the workbench and prepared to fill it in and sign it.

He printed in black ink "08 Archtop" in the model space and "2012   30" in the serial number space and asked me if I wanted the guitar named after me since it was a new design that we'd conceived together and that I'd commissioned.

I laughed, thinking he must be joking since signature model guitars are typically named after famous guitarists and I certainly wasn't one of those. He might have been serious, but I was embarrassed by the notion and instead suggested that we call it the "Westcoast Archtop," a suitable name, I thought, given the provenance of the woods and the place of construction. Robert agreed and printed in 'Westcoast.' With that, the guitar was named and the label glued in place.

It was time to assemble the body.

It's one thing to glue and clamp rectangular pieces

of wood together where all the surfaces are flat and the edges straight, but to me the curving, arching body of a guitar presented a unique challenge. I was curious to see how Robert would manage it.

It didn't take long to find out.

First he laid the back in a wooden cradle on his bench. The cradle, a shallow foam-lined box with a guitar-shaped hole cut out of the top, protected it from damage and held it in place.

Then he placed the sides – still in the mould – atop the back, aligning the entire assembly carefully and leaving a small bit of overlap around the perimeter of the back.

He then applied pressure to check the fit, not with the clamps I was expecting but with 'go-bars,' an ancient, low-tech clamping system that uses flexible sticks under tension to press the parts together.

To picture how these work imagine fitting a long flexible stick under a table, with one end on the floor and the other pushed up against the underside of the table. It stays in place because it's been flexed to fit.

Go-bars have been used for centuries to glue piano and harpsichord parts together, particularly when attaching braces to the large soundboards. With the soundboard placed on the floor of the workshop, the braces can be laid on top. Go-bars push down from the ceiling to hold them in place.

Modern guitar builders often use a go-bar deck, a box-like rig with a plywood top and base held together by four metal posts. The body is placed on the floor of the deck and the go-bars are fitted inside, pushing against the top and creating what looks like a cage with curved bars.

Robert used to employ this method but aways found that the posts and roof of the deck got in his way. He figured it made more sense to put the guitar parts on his bench and fit the bars against the ceiling, giving him unencumbered access from all sides – a scaled-down version of the piano technique.

And so he built a shallow rectangular plywood box with open ends and attached it to the ceiling above his bench. The box stores his go-bars (different sizes, all roughly three to four feet long) and provides the overhead surface for the bars to push against.

I watched as he moved freely around the setup, placing the go-bars, bending over to check the fit, and making small adjustments. To protect the thin edges of the sides and distribute the pressure more evenly, he'd laid a guitar-shaped piece of pegboard on top, creating a sandwich that consisted of the cradle, the guitar back, the sides still in the mould, and the pegboard protector.

Soon he had a dozen or so bars applying downward pressure on the entire assembly. Satisfied that the fit was good, he disassembled everything and turned to his pot of hide glue that had been heating on the counter by the sink. He applied the glue to the parts, reassembled everything and once again placed the go-bars.

The process took time and Robert thought it likely

the glue had set too soon. He explained that because hide glue is water-based, it can set before the pieces are properly fitted and clamped. Warm water can be applied to soften the glue, but that's a messy and time consuming process.

Robert had a simple solution – steam. Unlike water which takes a moment to soak in, steam will immediately wick into the molecules-wide space between the glued pieces and reactivate the glue instantly.

But how was he going to apply steam?

The answer was yet another of his improvised tools – a small steamer originally intended for cleaning spots off clothes and upholstery that he'd acquired for about twenty dollars at a local discount outlet. It was ridiculously simple, consisting of nothing more than a plastic container with a heating element, a trigger and a flexible hose.

He filled the container with water and plugged it in. He waited a minute and then pulled the trigger. Out shot a cloud of steam. It was ready to go.

He aimed the hose at the inside edge of each joint and began working his way around, shooting out billows of steam like a fumigator annihilating insects.

In minutes he was done.

In a few hours the glue would cure.

In a few days he'd repeat the go-bar process to attach the top. The joints produced would be stronger than the wood itself. Most important, the guitar body would be assembled and we could turn our attention to the neck. Our guitar-building train was heading for the next station.

Twenty-One

THE BODY WHOLE

Through much of my life I've enjoyed hiking and backpacking in the very mountains where the wood for my guitar grows. I've loved getting to know the lie and contour of the trails under my feet and the slow, steady, sometimes strenuous movement upwards from the deep evergreen forests of the valleys to the heather-rich meadows of the sub-alpine. At times the going is easy; at times it is tough. Always it is slow and purposeful, particularly under the weight of a heavy backpack.

In the valleys, the trails run beside creeks, rising gently mile by mile as they lead you further into the mountains. On the hillsides, they rise steeply, switchbacking up heavily forested slopes that offer few views by which you can gauge your progress.

You persist, moving slowly under the weight of your pack, stopping to snack and drink every hour or so to keep your energy up, stepping carefully over roots, rocks and other obstacles and climbing over or slipping under fallen trees that occasionally block the trail.

Eventually you break through onto an open

shoulder where you are rewarded with views of distant mountains, the valley you left behind, and the lake you passed earlier – now a thousand feet below – and you realize that you've made significant progress. You recognize that the patient and cumulative act of placing one foot after the other has taken you to a new state of being.

Life is like this and so too, it turns out, is guitar making. The early days are slow going, particularly when starting as we did with rough chunks of wood that require considerable preparation before one can even begin the slow process of carving the top and back.

Reflecting on those days, when Robert was filling a large plastic garbage can with wood shavings that piled up on the bench and floor of his workshop, I thought of my backpacking experiences. That's when we were lost in the trees, unable to see our progress or our destination. Now, with the guitar body sitting on the bench before us, we'd reached our first major goal. We'd emerged on a shoulder of our mountain and were seeing for the first time how far we'd come. One day soon, circumstances willing, we'd climb above the tree-line and reach the high ridges that lead to the final summit.

But we still had a ways to go.

The next step was to complete the final details of the guitar body. The top and back and sides were one unit now and the mould that had served as a form to shape it and hold it all together had been removed, but there were a few rough edges to take care of.

The edges of a guitar body are trimmed with thin strips of wood or synthetic material (usually plastic or celluloid) called binding. Like the baseboards and window casings of a house, its job is to fill gaps and create a finished look. It also provides a protective edge.

Sometimes you'll see highly decorative materials like mother-of-pearl used to bind a guitar. My inclination was to avoid fancy details that would conflict with our simple design ethic. Robert agreed and suggested koa, a species of Acacia, a mahogany-like hardwood grown in Hawaii that he felt would frame the lighter-toned spruce and maple nicely. It would be set off visually from the other woods with ultra-thin, multi-layered black and wood-toned purfling.

But the body needed more preparation first. Donning his dust mask and ear protectors, Robert turned to his table-mounted router to remove the protruding edges

of the top and back. These overhanging lips were created when he first cut out the top and back on his bandsaw, intentionally leaving an eighth of an inch of material beyond the pencil lines he'd traced using the mould as a template.

I was nervous at the thought of him taking a router to the body but he quickly and expertly steered it on the router table around the whirling bit and removed the material. Then he clamped the body in a large padded wood vice and used a scraper and sanding block to smooth the flush edges he'd created.

To install the binding and purfling Robert had to create a stepped ledge called a double rabbet around the top and bottom edges of the body. The binding would go on the deeper outside ledge and the narrow purfling on the shallower inside ledge. He explained that this task could be done with specialized hand tools but that it was much simpler and quicker to use his router and a special jig he'd created.

When he mentioned using the router yet again, a tool that could do a lot of damage if it slipped, I imagined it skipping across the top of the guitar, tearing and gouging the beautiful hand-carved spruce top as the two of us stood there in disbelief, realizing that we'd have to start over again.

I consciously stepped back from the bench to avoid getting in his way as he set up the jig for this operation. I certainly didn't want to be a distraction this late in the game.

The jig consisted of a small wheeled sled that could move freely atop his bench and a device that clamped the router to the side of the bench. Robert explained that rather than move the router around the body which could result in a slip, he'd move the body around the router. This way all he had to do was control the lateral movements and not worry about the depth of the cut since the router would be set at a pre-determined height. Knowing this, I relaxed slightly as he set the body on the sled and prepared to make the cuts.

But there was a problem. Testing the movement of the sled he discovered that part of the router jig was getting in the way. He'd designed it for flat-top guitars, but this was an archtop, with the arch creating extra height that prevented it from fitting under a clear plastic plate that was part of the jig. Robert pondered the problem for a moment and then with little hesitation pulled out a  small Japanese handsaw that cut by pulling rather than pushing and sawed off the offending piece of plastic. Apparently guitar making required not only skill but also the courage to reach for a quick and dirty solution when needed!

The whine and scream of the router – loud even with ear protection – unhinged me a little as Robert hunched over and pushed the body of the guitar toward the spinning blade. He got his eyes level with the top of the guitar and watched carefully as he edged it closer. Committed, he made the final push and the whirling blade cut in, spraying out shavings as he created a small test cut at the top of the guitar where the neck would be attached. A mistake here wouldn't matter since a dovetail joint would be created in this area and so any damage would be covered up by the fingerboard projecting over the top of the body. He pulled the body back to check his work. Dissatisfied with depth of the cut, he turned the router off and adjusted it.

This time the depth was right and soon wood shavings were blasting out, only to be sucked into the hose of his dust collection system mounted behind the router on the jig as he skillfully maneuvered the sled around the contour of the body. He completed one side, paused, and then set to work on the other.

He adjusted the router to cut the second ledge that would accommodate the purfling. This work also went smoothly and in minutes he was finished.

I could relax as he repeated the process on the back.

Before I knew it he was done. Where there had been rough joints, there were now finely cut ledges around the perimeter of the top and bottom of the body.

With the double rabbets cut top and back, he could now turn to heating, bending, and glueing the binding and purfling in place.

Over the course of an hour or so he used the same bending iron he'd employed to bend the sides and worked carefully, fitting the pieces onto the ledges and securing them with masking tape while the glue set.

With that work done, the body was complete except for the fine finishing that would come later.

It was time to move on to the next major stage of our journey up the mountain: building the neck.

Twenty-Two

THE NECK: PART ONE

Linda Manzer told me that carving a guitar neck is a "touchy-feely" thing. While she could measure to a certain degree, in the end it came down to how the neck felt in her hands and, more important, in the hands of the player. Over the years she'd come to know the shape of Pat Metheny's hand and the feel he wanted. But even with that knowledge it was tricky to get it right every time. She admitted to being nervous whenever she took him a new guitar because she could never be absolutely sure that it would be perfect. She had virtuosic control of her craft and years of experience, but the wood itself had its own way of being.

I thought about this as I drove along damp city streets on a cloudy, cold December afternoon to Robert's shop. How did I want the neck of my guitar to feel? How would Robert and I work together to find that feel? How much should I direct him and how much should I let him shape the neck as he saw fit? These and other questions tossed around in my head as I neared his house.

I stepped into the warmth of his shop to find him

already working with the neck blank on his bench. Made of Honduran mahogany, the blank was about thirty inches long, four inches wide and three inches thick with a stubby foot at one end. It looked more like a club than the neck of a guitar. He'd already drawn the rough profile of the neck in pencil and was getting ready to trim away the excess wood on his bandsaw.

Archtop guitar necks are often made with maple, either one solid piece or a few pieces laminated together. It's the same material you'll find most solid body electric guitar necks crafted from. Hard and stable, it's prized for its brightness, a desirable sonic quality in a rock or blues guitar and in an archtop crafted to step out front with fluid solo lines. But Robert had suggested mahogany, a warmer wood typically found on flat-top guitars and older acoustic archtops, because it was lighter than maple and fit with his philosophy of building the lightest, most responsive instrument possible. And being softer than maple, it was easier to carve.

I accepted his suggestion because I remembered a Godin solid-body electric guitar I'd owned that had a mahogany neck. That guitar had a lot of warmth and sustain, more than usual, and I thought that could only be a good thing on an archtop, an instrument that could sometimes be a tad brittle sounding. I wanted clarity but I also wanted warmth, and I hoped that combining mahogany with maple and spruce would yield the balance I sought.

The bandsaw jolted into action and Robert, with his yellow ear protectors on, bent over and guided the neck blank along the saw table, keeping the blurred line of the blade close to but not touching the pencil line he'd drawn. The blade cut smoothly through the mahogany and soon the club looked more like the neck it would become with the angled headstock now apparent at one end.

At the other still-stubby heel end, the part that would mate with the body, Robert used a protractor to measure and draw a line to indicate how much wood he needed to remove. Because it was very little, he used his bench-top belt sander rather than the saw, removing the material with a series of passes and checking each time with a small square until he was satisfied.

With the blank prepared, he was ready to complete several other steps before he started carving. The first, and to me the most frightening, was to cut the joint that would attach the neck to the body. On many solid-body electric guitars, the neck is bolted on. The neck heel fits into a pocket routed in the body and screws or bolts hold it in place. Acoustic guitars and some electrics typically use a set neck with a glued joint, either a dovetail or a standard mortise and tenon. Robert preferred the dovetail, a joint so old it predated written history and had been found on furniture entombed with Egyptian mummies and Chinese emperors. Traditionally it was made with a handsaw and chisel but Robert explained that he would use jigs he'd made for his flat-top guitars in combination with his router to cut the two parts of the joint. The trapezoidal male end – the dovetail – would be cut into the heel of the neck blank. That didn't worry me so much because we had invested relatively little time in the neck. He could always cut out a second blank. But the mortise, the female half, was a different story. It had to be cut into the heel block glued inside the body. We'd spent the better part of a year building that body. Once the cut was made that would be it. What if something went wrong? Could Robert repair it? I'd heard that dovetail joints were difficult to execute well.

The jig for cutting the dovetail was attached to one end of his bench. Into this he clamped the neck blank, heel end up against a cut-out square of plywood with an attached clear plastic template that would guide the router. Aligning the template with a centre line he'd drawn on the heel's face, he screwed the clear plastic plate right into the heel to ensure nothing would move. He then set the depth of his plunge router for the first cut, tightened the knobs, and positioned the router on the template.

"Okay, here we go."

One final check and the router whined to life as he switched it on and guided it into the wood, tracing the trapezoidal shape with a series of short strokes as the router's voice deepened and thickened and a vacuum hose sucked away the flying debris.

Several adjustments and a dozen strokes later, Robert was done. He unclamped the neck from the jig and held the heel end up to the light, examining the angled sides of the dovetail as he thumbed away a bit of sawdust.

Satisfied, he laid it down and turned his attention to the body at the far end of the bench.

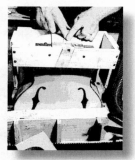

The setup for cutting the mortise was more elaborate. It involved Robert first clamping the body upright in a wood vice with thick foam inserts that protected it from damage. He then fit a jig – essentially a narrow rectangular plywood box with no bottom and two vertical side wings with screw clamps – over the upper half, encasing the body and providing a platform for the clear plastic template that would guide the routing. Robert spent considerable time adjusting and securing the whole assembly before finally aligning the plastic template and screwing it into the neck block.

"I think we're ready."

I stepped back and held my breath as he adjusted the router and set it atop the template. Setting his feet and steadying his hands, he switched it on and plunged the whirring bit into the guitar body. Sawdust flew as I stood tensely waiting to see the result. He switched off the router, placed it on the bench, and removed the body from the clamp.

The moment of truth had come. Would the dovetail fit snugly into the mortise and, most important, would the neck and body align?

Robert picked up the neck and tried fitting it to the body by gently coaxing the parts together. It wouldn't go. He took a small sanding block and stroked away a few rough edges on the dovetail. Still not right. He went back and forth like this a few times before he was finally able to coax the parts together. Finally the neck fit snugly: not tight, not loose – perfect.

I let out a breath.

There was one more thing to check.

He took a metre-long metal rule and laid it atop the assembled neck and body with the straight edge running from top to bottom. "I'm checking to see if the centrelines I've marked coincide," he explained, adding that if they were slightly off he'd have to compensate by making slight adjustments with shims. Holding the rule in place he angled the guitar up to the light  and tilted his head sideways. The rule slipped. He set it in place again and once again tilted his head and glanced up and down the guitar.

"Looks good. I think we've got it."

I relaxed.

I assumed we were now ready to start carving but I was wrong. More steps remained, steps we wouldn't complete on this day and some of which I wouldn't witness directly.

One was to make a small neck extension that would project over the body. On a flat-top guitar, the neck extends as one piece and is attached directly to the top. On an archtop the fingerboard projects above the top to allow free vibration, accommodate a steeper neck angle, and provide room for installing a floating pickup. To make this projection possible Robert had to craft a separate piece of mahogany that would attach to the underside of the fingerboard and the neck via a glued rabbet joint.

Another step was to cut a channel in the neck to accommodate a truss rod. Invented in the early twentieth century by Gibson, the truss rod, made of steel, runs the length of the neck underneath the fingerboard and has a bolt at one end that can be tightened or loosened to adjust the downward bow or 'relief' of the neck, making it possible to change the action. It also makes the neck considerably stronger.

Steel guitar strings exert well over a hundred pounds of tension, enough to bow a neck temporarily and warp it over time. The truss rod counteracts this tension, allowing a builder to make the neck thinner and hence more playable.

Nylon string guitar necks usually don't employ a truss rod because gut or nylon strings exert much less tension and the necks are wider and thicker as befits the style of play and conventions of the instrument.

Robert also had to make and attach the fingerboard. Typically constructed of maple, rosewood or ebony,

the fingerboard, along with the neck, is the most intimate part of a guitar, the place where the fretting fingers
form chords and find melodies, sliding and slurring,
hammering on and hammering off, and shifting in time
with the rhythmic demands of the right hand and its
volley of strums, plucks and sweeps. The fingerboard
has to feel good under the fingers for this to happen
smoothly. It has to feel right to make coordination with
the plucking and strumming hand possible. It can't be
too wide or too narrow, too flat or too curved. And it
has to be mathematically precise to ensure that the right
notes will sound.

I'd already told Robert that my preference for material
was ebony. I loved its look and feel. It was so dense,
tightly grained and smooth, that even left unfinished, it
looked polished, exuding a warmth and richness that in
my mind surpassed rosewood and maple.

Ebony grows in several parts of the world, including
Africa, Sri Lanka and Indonesia and has a long human
history. Carved ebony artifacts have been found in
Egyptian tombs, and it was used by the kings of India
for drinking cups they believed would counteract
poison. It's the wood traditionally used to make the
black keys of a piano, the black pieces of a chess set, and
the pins, chin rests and tailpieces of violins. It inspired
the wonderful French word for cabinetmaker, ébéniste,
after Parisian woodworkers began making carved
ebony cabinets for the fine European furniture trade
in the sixteenth century. Today it even has a virtual

presence in the form of the medieval blades, mail and maces found in some popular role-playing video games.

Cutting and slotting the fingerboard is the most critical operation because there's no room for even a slight error. The length has to be precise and the slots cut to accommodate the frets have to be perfectly spaced to ensure that when a string is depressed the right note will sound. Fretboard construction is mathematical not intuitive.

Pythagoras is credited with first understanding that the length of a vibrating string determines its pitch and that the relationship between two pitches can be expressed as a mathematical ratio. He conducted experiments with a monochord, an instrument invented by the Greeks that consisted of a sound box with a single string stretched between two points. A moveable bridge could be placed and shifted under the string to create different notes. When he set the bridge in the middle, thus shortening the string by half, the note that sounded was an octave higher than the open string note because it was vibrating at twice the frequency. The ratio therefore was 1:2. When he moved the bridge to other locations he got different notes and different mathematical results, eventually figuring out all the ratios associated with the Western even-tempered scale.

On a guitar the octave note of a string is found at the twelfth fret because that fret is located halfway between the nut and the bridge. Moving up the fingerboard from the nut, each fret takes us a semitone (half-step) closer to that octave note. The Benedetto book has a table showing the distances between frets for a twenty-five-inch scale length with twenty-one frets. (Scale length refers to the length of the string between the nut and the bridge.) With this scale length, fret one is 1.403 inches from the nut. Fret two is 1.324 inches from fret one. Fret three is 1.250 inches from fret two. The fret positions are that precise. No deviation. No error.

It is possible to make the measurements and cut the slots by hand. In practice most luthiers use templates, jigs and power tools to accomplish this task.

Robert would use a slotting jig he'd designed to work with his table saw. He would mount the blank in the jig and make progressive passes on the saw to cut the slots. With the slots cut, he could then taper the fingerboard, making it progressively wider from top to bottom. This taper allows the spacing between the strings to widen up the neck. Otherwise there would be little room for the fingers of the plucking hand.

He would also cut an attractive contour at the end of the fingerboard instead of chopping it off flat. This was a design feature I really liked. It added flair without being excessive.

He would inlay the abalone dots that marked the frets at various positions along the fingerboard. These fret markers are both decorative and functional. A fretted instrument can become a visual blur when you're in the throes of playing. It's helpful to have landmarks that identify the fret positions. Robert offered me the possibility of fancier markers, but for aesthetic and financial reasons, I chose simple dots. Other designs would require considerably more time to cut out and inlay. With the pre-cut dots he could drill the holes, apply glue and pop them in.

After all this the fingerboard would be ready to be glued to the neck, thus covering the truss rod already mounted in its channel. Once the glue had set Robert would be free to sand in the radius, the arch in the fingerboard that accommodates the natural curvature of the fingers to make playing easier. The smaller the radius the greater the arch; the larger the radius the more flat the fingerboard. The trick is to find a balance. Small radius fretboards enhance rhythm playing because they make it easier to 'barre' a chord. Large radius fretboards make single line and fingerstyle playing easier. Classical guitars, which are designed almost exclusively for fingerstyle playing, usually have a completely flat fingerboard for this reason.

The radius can be either simple or compound (conical). Like the top of a cylinder, a simple radius is consistent all the way along the fretboard. If it's a twelve-inch radius at the nut, it's twelve inches at the body. A compound radius changes. It's more like the top of a cone with more curve at the nut end and gradually less curve towards the body.

Some builders consider the compound or conical radius superior because the gradual change is intended to create the best of both worlds, making chording easy near the nut, and single line playing easier as you move up the neck. It also ensures that the string height or action will be consistent the full length of the fretboard. Robert favoured a compound radius.

Ultimately each decision is a personal choice. As Linda Manzer said, you could measure things to a certain degree but in the end it came down to how it all felt in the hands of the player.

I was content to follow Robert's lead on many of these decisions. As we'll see in the next chapter I probably should have been a little more proactive with this process.

Twenty-Three

THE NECK: PART TWO

The construction of the neck reflected an unspoken and unfelt tension in our project. I say unfelt because I really wasn't aware of it at the time. Like Robert I was immersed in the day-to-day progress. Only later did Robert's partner Susan mention it as something she was aware of and that might make an interesting theme in the book.

Inevitably I saw the guitar we were building as an instrument that would suit my needs and desires. Just as inevitably Robert saw it as a prototype, a model that could be the basis for future guitars he might build. As such he had certain features he wanted to include while still meeting my needs. Because he was clearer in his mind about some of these details – everything from fingerboard width, to scale length, to fingerboard radius, to fret size, to neck profile – his ideas tended to carry more weight.

I had thought about asking him to duplicate the neck dimensions and features of an electric archtop I owned and liked a lot (a Yamaha AEX 1500 built in the early nineties and designed by guitarist Martin Taylor) but didn't feel strongly enough to push the idea. I went back and forth in my own mind about it and so didn't have a clear vision of what I wanted. Also I respected his knowledge and was willing to follow his lead.

We did discuss these matters somewhat but I don't recall a detailed consideration of all the individual features of the neck and fingerboard that we would incorporate. If we'd had that discussion, I likely still would have deferred to Robert.

In hindsight I might have asked for a slightly narrower fingerboard or at least one with slightly more arch to accommodate my fingers which are relatively short. As well, I might have requested a shorter scale length to reduce the string tension – likely a twenty-five inch scale as opposed to slightly the longer one Robert favoured. Mostly, though, I would have gone with his suggestions – except for one feature that will become obvious as the story unfolds.

Before he began carving the neck, Robert still had to complete several other steps. He cut the piece of ebony veneer that would face the headstock and inlaid his stylized logo into that veneer. After glueing the veneer to the face of the headstock, he shaped the headstock with a router and bound the fingerboard and headstock with strips of koa. He cut and hammered in pieces of brass fret wire into the fingerboard slots and filed the frets. He bound the fingerboard. Essentially he completed everything about the neck and fingerboard except the carving.

Of all the tasks, the most interesting in many ways was the inlaying of the headstock logo, a thin piece of abalone cut in a stylized art nouveau figure derived from Robert's initials "RA." Designed by a graphic artist, it was a simple but classy design, but it was so thin and delicate I had no idea how he would inlay it. Tracing the shape onto to the face of the veneer didn't seem possible given the logo's intricacy and fragility. Without an

accurate outline, how would he remove the precise shape and amount of wood from the veneer to make insetting the logo possible?

The answer was a jig he'd fashioned that used a plastic moulding material and a rotary cutting tool. Robert spread the moulding material on one side of the jig and attached the piece of ebony veneer to the other. He then pressed the abalone logo into the moulding material with a small tool and allowed it to set. When he gently removed the logo several minutes later, an imprint was left behind.

He then attached a movable clear plastic plate over the jig. One side was fitted with a pin designed to trace the moulded imprint and the other side held the rotary cutting tool above the veneer. Cutting the logo shape was then as easy as guiding the pin around the imprint while the rotary tool etched the identical shape into the face of the veneer. Robert's jig was a variation of a pantograph, a device invented in 1603 that traces an image with one pen, while duplicating it with another – essentially a mechanical CNC (computer numerical control) machine. I marvelled at the simplicity and effectiveness of it.

In modern factories guitar necks are shaped in minutes by CNC machines. The blank is clamped into place and the cutting head zips back and forth, profiling the shape into the blank, leaving only final finishing to be done by hand.

Robert estimated that by using hand tools – primarily a spokeshave, finger plane and scraper – it would take him a week to complete the neck, working a couple of hours each day.

He proposed a 'vintage V' profile, a shape that appeared on guitar necks before the development of  the truss rod. V-shaped necks evolved from the rounded necks typical of classical guitars because they could withstand the heavier tension of steel strings without warping. At the same time hand comfort was improved because the neck was less bulky.

As truss rods and lighter strings became standard, the V-neck gave way to the slimmer profiles found on most modern guitars. A slimmer neck generally means greater comfort and playing ease but Robert favoured the 'V' (a 'soft V' with a rounded bottom) partly because of tradition and partly because he felt it gave a fingerstyle player more stability by providing a solid base for the thumb to brace against when moving up and down the neck and reaching for notes. Eric Schoenberg, who had contracted Robert to build guitars for his Tiburon shop, also liked it and so Robert was accustomed to producing this shape on his instruments.

I'd never owned a guitar with a V-profile before but in the spirit of adventure I was willing to give it a try. I'd played one of Robert's flat-tops and could feel how the V did provide a fulcrum for the thumb, particularly when I cocked my wrist to reach across the fingerboard. I decided to leave him to it, planning to return to the shop when he was done the initial carving.

The day came when the neck was ready to try. Robert had fitted it to the body without glueing the dovetail joint so I could mimic playing and feel it under my fingers. I cradled the guitar in my lap and began running my left hand up and down the neck, feeling the 'V' under my thumb and noting how it aided or impeded my fingering of imaginary chords. I carried on for some time. I paused, reflected and discussed what I was feeling with Robert and tried it again. As I grew more familiar with the neck, I began noticing occasional inconsistencies here and there, places where it didn't feel quite right or where I could feel a slight bump. I mentioned these issues to Robert, and as they came up, he would take the guitar from me and tend to the area I'd identified with a scraper and sanding block. He would then hand it back and I would try again.

We went back and forth like this before we narrowed it down to one final problem that I felt needed attention: the area near the heel of the guitar felt too thick when I attempted to reach notes above the twelfth fret near the body joint. Jokingly referred to by guitarists as the 'dusty end,' this area isn't typically visited by acoustic guitar players but it is common to play jazz chords up there and so it was important to get it right. The heel had to be thick enough to ensure strength, while still allowing a comfortable grip and easy movement. Robert acknowledged that he could take more wood off if I left it with him, which I did, returning a day or two later to discover that all was well and the neck felt smooth from top to bottom.

I wasn't totally in tune with the 'V' but felt with time I'd get used to it and would eventually grow to like it. I was mistaken.

Twenty-Four

FRENCH POLISHING

Not long after he carved the neck Robert called to say he was ready to start finishing the guitar. It was hard to believe that we'd begun the process a year before and now, having done the final sanding of the entire instrument, he was about to bring out the natural beauty of the wood by employing a process called French polishing. His plan was to finish the neck and body with this method before glueing them together and attaching the tailpiece, bridge, and strings to complete the guitar.

The end of our project was finally in sight.

French polishing is a process that uses plant shellac, plant resins and other materials dissolved in alcohol to produce a gloss finish. The materials are mostly rubbed on rather than sprayed or brushed. Its provenance seems uncertain, with some writers attributing it to early nineteenth-century France, others to the eighteenth century, and others still insisting that it dates back to Renaissance Italy, where they say it was first used to finish fine furniture and later musical instruments. In any case French polishing is appreciated for its ability to bring out not only the natural beauty of tonewood but also its acoustical properties since it results in a very thin finish that allows the wood to vibrate freely, unlike some of the heavier synthetic finishes commonly used on guitars today that tend to restrict the natural vibrations.

It's a labour-intensive process requiring hours of work, and for that reason it fell out of favour with the advent of the factory production of guitars, which demanded faster methods of finishing. It was superseded as early as the 1920s by nitrocellulose, a spray-on lacquer developed for the auto industry. Nitrocellulose is a solvent-based finish created by blending cellulose – usually cotton – with nitric and sulphuric acid – the same process used to create nitroglycerin, TNT and other explosive materials. It was valued because it blended well with paint and dried quickly, allowing successive layers to be sprayed on over a short period of time. But it's also highly flammable and toxic and so was largely replaced in the seventies by less dangerous polyurethane finishes commonly used today.

While the factory guitar world abandoned French polishing, violin and other classical instrument makers continued to use it, as did some individual guitar builders. Robert initially adopted it to avoid the toxicity of the more modern finishes. He tried tung oil and acrylic lacquer on his first two guitars. Unhappy with the results, he turned to French polishing at the suggestion of double bass builder Jim Ham. Ham invited him to a session with Greg Brown, an expert in the technique who was about to start finishing a double bass Ham was building for Gary Karr, an internationally known classical bassist who lives in Victoria. After observing Brown and trying his own hand at it, Robert watched an instructional video issued by a lutherie supply company, experimented further, and then began employing it himself.

But he had problems. It turns out there is more than one French polishing method. The one described in the video created a finish susceptible to heat damage, which he discovered when he shipped his first French-polished guitars to California. They sat in a hot warehouse in the interior of the state for customs processing before being sent on to Eric Schoenberg's shop on the coast. The guitars arrived with finish damage which Robert had to repair.

He described the problem to Marcus Dominelli, a classical guitar builder in Victoria, who suggested taking a course from Geza Burghardt, a master luthier in Vancouver who builds guitars and works on stringed instruments owned by members of the Vancouver Symphony Orchestra. Burghardt left Hungary in the eighties before the fall of the Iron Curtain, and brought with him old world techniques used on European classical instruments. Robert contacted Burghardt, who assured him, that if he took his course, "All of your problems will be over."

The first step in French polishing as taught by

Burghardt is to prepare the wood by using egg white applied with a brush and smoothed with a damp cloth.

"You can't get more organic than that," I joked to Robert when he showed me the egg whites he'd cracked into a small jar in his kitchen that morning.

"And they're from free range chickens," he countered as he dipped in his dampened brush and began applying the albumen with short, fast strokes, quickly covering the top of the guitar before using a damp cloth to smooth it. As the egg white went on, the spruce top darkened and the grain began to emerge. The effect was even more pronounced when he turned to the sides and back, where the figure in the maple, previously faint, leaped out.

Egg white, known as "vernice bianca" (white varnish) to the Italians, acts as a sealer, creating a ground for the next phase in the process. Many violin builders believe it is key to the tone enhancement attributed to French-polished instruments. Some even advocate applying it to the inside of the body.

Simone Fernando Sacconi (1895-1973), a famous modern violin maker who studied Stradivari's techniques extensively and wrote a book on the subject called *The Secrets of Stradivari* – which has influenced contemporary violin builders – believed that vernice bianca was one of the elements that made Stradivari violins sound so good. The recipe in his book calls for the addition of gum arabic, honey, rock candy and water, all combined in precise measurements and prepared in a particular way. Robert's recipe was simpler – just plain egg white – but he said the alcohol used as a carrier for the other ingredients he'd apply later – shellac, various resins, fine sawdust and pumice – would dissolve everything, including the egg white, into one substance that he believed had a similar effect.

As the sealer went on, it raised the grain in areas that needed more finishing or that had been compressed by tool damage. He sanded these areas with progressively finer sandpaper and then rubbed them with a cloth. The goal was to get the surface as flat and smooth as possible.

He applied a second coat of sealer, this time with a drop of amber vegetable die added and continued looking for raised or rough areas that needed attention.

He explained that less detailed sanding and rubbing would be needed on the sides and back because maple, being harder, was less susceptible to tool damage and grain raising.

Once the surface was sealed and smooth, Robert turned to filling the wood pores by using a 'pounce bag,' a knotted cloth filled with wadded cotton and pumice, the crystalline dust of volcanoes. Pounce bags are filled with everything from fine cuttlebone to sandarac to charcoal and used by calligraphers to 'size' their paper and by artists to transfer patterns onto a new surface. Robert was using pumice because as he patted it on the surface and rubbed it in with an alcohol soaked rag, it abraded the wood slightly, creating an ultra-fine sawdust that mixed with the pumice and egg white to fill the pores.

Once he was satisfied, he turned to priming the surface by applying a diluted mixture of rubbing alcohol, shellac, various resins, and a drop of amber dye. All the while he continued looking for areas of raised grain or compression that he'd missed. He sanded and rubbed, rubbed and sanded and held the guitar body up to the light repeatedly to check for areas that needed more attention.

As the afternoon ticked by it was clear to me that in Robert's hands French polishing was no slap-dash affair. He was like a jeweler polishing the surface of a valuable gem or more prosaically, a hyper-conscientious window cleaner intent on removing every last spot and streak down to the molecular level. Through Robert's patient work, the spruce top got progressively smoother and was eventually ready for the first application of the shellac and other resins that would create the gloss finish.

I recall seeing cans of shellac on shelves in the basement of my childhood home and in the hardware stores I've frequented all my life. I even used it on one of my first woodworking projects in high school, a carved yellow cedar tray with mahogany ends I made in grade nine.

I've always assumed that it was some kind of petroleum product like most other substances we finish wood with these days. When Robert was ready to mix his formula and began explaining its origin, and later when I did more research, I discovered I didn't know shellac at all.

In South Asia a small red parasitic scale insect called the "lac bug" swarms in vast numbers on certain trees twice a year (known colloquially as 'lac' trees), and feeds on sap extracted by penetrating the bark with its proboscis. Numbering in the tens of thousands on a single branch, they literally kill themselves by overeating during this 'feast of death,' all the while excreting a resin which dries and forms a hard shell that encrusts and protects the whole colony. It's a Dionysian orgy, with the males fertilizing the females before dying off and the females excreting more and more resin to protect the eggs they'll lay before they too pass on. The eggs hatch into larvae, and the larvae grow into young insects which break through the crust to move on and begin the process anew.

Local villagers harvest the encrusted branches and take them to processing facilities where the resin is scraped off, ground by millstones, heated, and forced through screens which filter out insect and plant debris. The resin dries and is further refined, going through several steps until a pure product is produced in thin sheets that are then broken into flakes. These refined flakes are turned into shellac by mixing them with ethyl alcohol, a process that happens either in a manufacturing facility, or in the case of my guitar, Robert's shop.

Shellac has been used for at least three thousand years and is even featured in the world's longest literary work, the *Mahabaratha*, the epic Sanskrit tale which, in the course of its 1.8 million words (three times longer than the Bible) tells the story of the Pandavas and the Kauravas, warring factions of the royal Kuru clan who inhabited northern India in the Iron (Vedic) age a few thousand years BCE. During a plot to get rid of the Pandavas, the Kauravas contract an architect to build a palace of flammable materials with lac and ghee (clarified butter), where Kunti, the Queen mother of the Pandavas, will be invited to stay and be burned. Kunti and her family members, warned by an uncle, escape and eventually the Pandavas are victorious.

Robert pulled out a small digital scale and began measuring the ingredients. He was guarded about the exact formula – not wanting to give it away – but acknowledged it was roughly three measures of shellac flakes to one measure of the other resins, including sandarac, gum mastic, and gum benzoin. Like shellac, these resins come in yellowish chips, flakes, tears or buttons which he stored in small plastic bags. Of the three, sandarac seems to be the most important because it has a higher melting point than shellac and imparts a hardness that prevents the kind of heat damage his guitars suffered from with the other method he'd used.

Scraped from cypress trees in North Africa – most notably Morocco – sandarac has a storied history reaching back at least to the middle ages. It was used as a remedy for diarrhea, as an incense, and as a varnish, a use that continues to this day. Calligraphers still use a powdered form to sprinkle on paper or vellum as a 'resist,' to control the ink and produce a finer line. Similarly, gum benzoin, harvested from balsam trees in Indonesia, has past and present uses in perfumery, incense-making and medicine. It's appealing scent is familiar to users of Friar's Balsam, a tincture used to treat skin conditions and in wilderness first aid to apply to the skin to ensure that blister dressings stick inside sweaty hiking boots.

Gum mastic has perhaps the most interesting background. The ancient Egyptians used it for embalming, and it's an essential ingredient in chrism, the holy oil used for anointing parishioners in the Orthodox church. It was used as a snakebite remedy, to fill teeth, prevent digestive problems, treat colds and freshen the breath. During the Ottoman period in Turkey, gum mastic was so valuable the penalty for stealing it was execution by order of the Sultan. In 1822, during the Greek War of Independence, the Ottomans slaughtered thousands of people on the Island of Chios, where it is primarily collected, but the Sultan spared the citizens in southern Chios where the mastic shrubs grow so they could continue supplying him and his harem (presumably for breath freshening before sex).

A modern study published in the New England Journal of Medicine suggests that its antibacterial properties may be useful in treating peptic ulcers by killing the Helicobacter pylori bacteria believed responsible for this affliction. Today the European Union protects the production of mastic on Chios and on the nearby Turkish coast. Harvesting takes place from July to October, when incisions are made in the trees and the mastic is allowed to drip onto the ground where it hardens into "Tears of Chios" and is collected.

Robert ground his resins in a coffee grinder, mixed them with heated rubbing alcohol, and then heated and cooled the solution three times before it reached a state where it could be applied. He applied it not with a brush, but with a pad called a 'menuca' consisting of cotton wadding covered with cotton cloth that soaked up the solution and allowed him to work methodically  using horizontal and diagonal strokes that ensured even coverage. The alcohol in the solution dissolved the shellac and egg white already on the surface, producing a unified film that could be easily repaired should the need arise.

As he worked in the quiet of his shop I kept thinking of him as an alchemist transforming not lead to gold but wood to sound. The names of the resins, their countries of origin, their mythological past and their cultural history all combined to generate an aura of romance around the finishing of my guitar.

Twenty-Five

THE EXPLODING GUITAR

On a bright early March day, I cycled along Victoria's Galloping Goose Trail across the historic Selkirk Trestle, enjoying the warm air, the sunlight glinting off the water, and the pure leg-stretching joy of bumping over this rebuilt ninety-seven-year-old wooden-decked structure that arches across the Gorge Waterway into Vic West where Robert's home and workshop are located.

Walkers, joggers and other cyclists streamed towards me, some in shorts, some in shirtsleeves, many wearing sunglasses for the first time in months. We were all enlivened by the fresh air and the promise of spring after the cloudy, cold and often rainy days we'd endured through the winter.

Robert had emailed to say that he was ready to carve the bridge and when that was done we could string up the guitar. I was surprised to get the email because the last time we'd met, after finishing the French polishing, he was still working on carving the ebony tailpiece and hadn't yet installed the tuners on the headstock. I'd expected it would be some time before we would be this close to actually completing the guitar.

I reached the far side of the trestle and powered up a dirt trail that took me through a park and onto the roadway that leads past turn-of-the-century homes to Robert's property. When I walked through the garden gate and into the warmth of the workshop and greeted Robert, I was stopped in my tracks by the sight of my guitar lying complete on his worktable. Not only were the tuners installed and the tailpiece finished but a bridge was done too – he'd already carved it! My eyes went immediately from it to the ebony-veneered headstock with Robert's stylized abalone logo glinting in the sunlight streaming through the window. And below the logo the small, graceful koa truss rod cover that tied in perfectly with the koa binding of the neck and body. And on down the ebony fingerboard with brass fret wire to the warm spruce top and maple sides glossy and lovingly polished. It was enough to take my breath away.

"So, are you ready to string it up?" Robert asked with more than a little anticipation in his voice.

"Yeah!" I answered as he explained that the bridge he'd carved was a temporary prototype that would eventually be replaced.

"Should we put on phosphor bronze or bright bronze strings?"

Walk into any guitar store and the string choices are overwhelming since there are many manufacturers and options. Phosphor bronze strings consist of a high carbon steel wire core wrapped with a 92% copper and 8% tin alloy with a little phosphorous and zinc thrown in for good measure. Invented in the seventies by the D'Addario string company, phosphor bronze offers, according to manufacturers, a "bright bell-like tone" with some warmth and richness mixed in. They are the most common strings found on acoustic guitars today because of their sound and because they are less subject to corrosion, lasting longer than bright bronze strings, which are typically made from 80% copper and 20% zinc, a combination that is said to yield a brighter sound, although opinions on this vary.

Other options exist, too, with different alloys in the wrap and even different cores, including a silk and steel combination that is well suited to smaller-bodied folk guitars played with a lighter touch. Nickel-plated steel is the favoured wrap for electric guitar strings and even for those rare acoustic guitars with magnetic pickups because both nickel and steel are ferrous metals that respond well to the magnetic field generated by a pickup, creating a stronger tone. Modern manufacturers have even come out with coated strings that resist corrosion, including gore-tex coated Elixir strings favoured by players like Martin Taylor, who value not only their longevity but also the reduced finger noise and already-broken-in-sound they produce right out of the package.

As well as materials, players take into account the gauge of the strings (from light to heavy), depending on their instrument and playing style. Lighter gauge strings are favoured by fingerstyle players using smaller-bodied instruments, whereas players with big dreadnought guitars pounding out a strong rhythm or seeking a heavy bass sound are likely to use a heavier gauge.

In the early days of the jazz archtop, players like Eddie Lang and Freddie Green depended on heavy strings because their instruments were not amplified. Using an adjustable bridge on their guitars, they'd raise the strings high off the fingerboard and get a strong chunky sound.

I chose the phosphor bronze strings Robert offered since they were the strings I knew and seemed to be the ones most generally recommended. Before he began installing them, he offered me a caution:

"It's going to take at least half an hour before the guitar starts to open up and you hear some richness in the sound. Mostly you'll hear just the strings at the beginning, but then as the body begins to resonate, some of the other colours and tones will start to come in. It's a fascinating process that I've seen time and again. So don't be disappointed at first."

Vintage acoustic guitars produced by companies like Gibson and Martin are highly valued because they've had years to open up and produce a full rich sound. I had my first experience of this a few years ago when I took a lesson from Joey Smith, a well-regarded bassist and guitarist from Tennessee who toured with and wrote arrangements for the Glenn Miller Orchestra before arriving in Victoria on a cruise ship and deciding to stay put. Joey has an old Gibson archtop which he invited me to play during the lesson and it quite literally blew my mind. When you play a good acoustic guitar, you can feel the vibrations against your chest. With this guitar I could feel them in my whole body and they seemed to extend into the floor and the air around me. For the first time I really understood why players valued these old guitars. They produce amazing tone with almost no effort.

Modern-day luthiers, with their refined building techniques, can produce that effect much earlier in the life of the instrument but it can go wrong too. Robert told me that if the guitar hadn't opened up after the first half hour, then we'd have to see how it was after a couple of weeks. If it still hadn't improved then we might have a 'bad' guitar on our hands and would have to start over again. I was sure he was being overly cautious – he did, after all, have a reputation for building responsive instruments – but then again this was his first archtop.

Robert laid the guitar on his bench and started stringing it up, alternating strings to hold the bridge in place, because, unlike a flat-top guitar that has a fixed bridge, the archtop bridge is movable and can be shifted to adjust the intonation. One by one the strings went on, and soon he was tightening them with the tuners to increase the tension and bring them up to pitch. With each turn he tested the string by plucking it and we began to hear the first tentative sounds of the guitar.

Strings put significant stress not only on the body but also the neck. A set of six steel strings can exert from one hundred to four hundred pounds of cumulative pressure when tightened and tuned, depending on the specific characteristics of the instrument and the nature of the strings. That's like having a one hundred to four hundred pound man hanging off the end of your guitar.

Robert continued to tighten the strings, subtly adjusting the bridge placement to get the intonation right and periodically checking the alignment of the strings in relation to the ebony tailpiece. He'd attached the tailpiece with a bracket he'd designed made of thin brass that was secured by an ebony end pin set by friction in a hole drilled in the end of the guitar. The brass piece attached to the tailpiece with a dovetail slot and was held in place by two brass pins.

He tightened the strings further, getting them closer and closer to pitch. We heard the odd creak as the tension increased and the strings exerted more pressure. Another turn, another creak, and then suddenly a SNAP and TWANG that startled both of us. The tailpiece broke away from the endpin, shot across the guitar and banged into the polished top before it bounced off and fell to the side, dangling from the intertwined strings.

My heart stopped as we surveyed the damage. The top had sustained a small dent and a few scratches. Robert was confident he could remove them and turned to examining the tailpiece to see what had happened.

The pins had failed and the brass piece had come right out of the dovetail slot. Robert pulled out the ebony end pin and removed the brass fitting. He looked at it briefly, declared it a failed prototype and put it aside.

Fortunately we'd already discussed and planned for a second method of attachment – a Sacconi tailpiece adjuster. Used on violins, cellos and other classical stringed instruments, it was a short, looped nylon cord with threaded ends and knurled brass nuts that made adjustment possible.

Benedetto recommends this method in his book but Robert had done further research through other luthiers and learned that many believe a full metal attachment produces a superior sound even though the adjuster is aesthetically more pleasing and simpler to install since it loops unobtrusively over the end pin. We'd planned to compare both methods but now only one was open to us.

Robert threaded the adjuster through two holes in the tailpiece that he'd drilled in preparation. He looped it over the end pin, reinstalled the strings and bridge and handed the guitar to me, suggesting I slowly bring it up to pitch. Nervous, I held it in playing position in my lap and began turning the tuners gradually Robert had done and plucking the strings with the fingers of my right hand. The strings tightened, the pitch rose and the guitar creaked. I looked at Robert. He looked at the tailpiece and declared it stable.

I turned the tuners a little more, bringing the strings

210

closer to pitch. More creaks. I looked at Robert again. "It's fine," he said, "keep going." One more turn, another creak and CRACK...TWANG...the tailpiece broke away again and slammed into my right hand, spanking the guitar top with a ringing SMACK.

I rubbed my stinging hand.

Robert stared in disbelief.

This time the ebony end pin had snapped, leaving the broken-off stub jammed in the hole and the tailpiece with the attached adjuster and twisted strings hanging uselessly off the side of the guitar.

After Robert examined the guitar top and discovered that the damage was once again minor and easily repaired, the only way we could respond was to start making jokes.

"I guess you're glad I wasn't filming this," I said.

"Yeah, you'd have blackmail material and it would be up on YouTube, ruining my reputation as a luthier."

"That's right. In fact, Robert, I want you to build me five more guitars and I'm not paying for any of them. Oh, and remember I was going to call the book *The Perfect Guitar?* I'm changing it to *The Exploding Guitar.*"

Robert pondered the broken end pin again. "I still can't believe it broke."

He turned to the Benedetto book just to confirm that Benedetto used ebony end pins and sure enough they were pictured in the text.

We considered different theories.

"Well, it was a violin end pin and violins don't have

nearly the same tension on the strings," said Robert.

"Maybe it just had a flaw or maybe there's more string pressure than we thought," I suggested.

The last idea made the most sense to me since the cord of the Sacconi adjuster would concentrate all the string pressure at one spot on the end pin. In any case, we had a problem and I was about to leave it with Robert to sort out, when he produced a bone end pin from a drawer and said, "This has got to be strong enough."

I looked at him skeptically but he insisted on pushing ahead, and so once again he laid the guitar on the work table, removed the broken-off ebony endpin and replaced it with the bone one. He refitted the bridge, adjusted the strings and started tightening. Convinced it was going to break again, I rolled my chair back when he picked up the guitar and held it in playing position to bring the strings up to pitch.

"What's the matter, don't you have any faith?"

"Yeah, but I'm just not sure what forces are at work here."

Robert tightened the strings. I awaited the third explosion.

It never came. The bone end pin held and before long he had the guitar tuned and was playing it.

The first sounds I heard were good but not great. After a few minutes he handed it to me. I played for a few minutes. Still nothing sensational.

We continued like this for half an hour, passing the guitar back and forth. And then suddenly, while Robert was playing a chord melody arrangement of "Over the Rainbow," I began to hear a difference. It was as if he'd flicked a switch.

Just as he'd predicted, the notes were richer, the bass had opened up, and I was getting excited.

After more than a year and a few hundred hours of work, my guitar was almost finished and was coming to life.

Twenty-Six

A KIND OF PERFECTION

I left the guitar with Robert so he could repair the damage to the top and carve a new tailpiece and bridge. He'd decided the tailpiece should be shorter and since he wouldn't be using the brass fitting, it no longer needed a dovetail slot. The failure of the prototype provided the opportunity to refine his design.

The bridge design was fine but he needed to fine tune it and carve it in ebony instead of the maple he'd used for the prototype. In keeping with his building philosophy, he'd opted for a lightweight, low-mass single-piece bridge without metal adjusters. He didn't want anything interfering with the transmission of the string vibrations to the top.

A week or so later Robert called to say the work was finished. The top was repaired, the new tailpiece mounted, the bridge completed and the guitar ready to pick up.

On a warm spring day I drove to Vic West and brought my new guitar home for the first time. As is always the case with a new instrument, I sat on the couch in the living room and played everything I knew repeatedly for a few hours – "All of Me," "Blue Bossa," "Satin Doll," "Autumn Leaves," "Alone Together," "Moonglow" and other jazz standards with chord changes I love to play.

Once again – this time under my own fingers – I heard the rich sounds that emerged when Robert played "Over the Rainbow" in his workshop. (Later I would learn that he always brought a new guitar into the world by playing that song. The sentiments expressed in the lyrics and the music seemed to fit his romantic, idealistic nature and capture his goals as a guitar maker. It was a nice tradition he'd established. The ideal made real.)

I noticed, too, the evenness of the sound from top to bottom, something Pat Metheny had talked about in relation to Linda Manzer's guitars. That consistency was present in Robert's instrument. The bass never overpowered, the treble never got too thin or twangy. Even the highest treble notes had a richness, a complexity that made them sound warm. And the mid-range was clear, not muddy. Through the whole tonal range, the notes were almost bell-like.

But something was wrong. As I played, I noticed the joint at the base of my thumb getting sore, something that had never happened with other guitars. Only one thing could explain it – the 'V' profile of the neck. All my other guitars had slimmer profiles. The neck Robert had carved with such care wasn't anatomically suited to my hand.

For the next few days I tried to find a comfortable

playing position that would relieve the pain but couldn't. However I positioned my hand, the discomfort would appear within a few minutes.

Just a few days after bringing the guitar home, I was back in Robert's shop and he was carving down the neck with spokeshave and scraper, removing the 'V' and slimming it to something more akin to a modern "D" shape.

The advantages of the French polish technique he'd used to finish the guitar came to the fore here. If he'd used a polyurethane finish, he would have had to remove all of the original finish on the neck before re-carving. With French polishing he could easily blend the newly carved area into the old, leaving no sign that new carving had been done.

We spent a couple of hours at this task. I was amazed at how quickly and expertly he was able to change the profile. We passed the guitar back and forth many times as he refined the shape. Soon it felt right and I was confident he could go ahead with a final sanding and refinishing.

Within the week, the job was finished and the guitar was finally done. My archtop could come home for the final time.

It's been nearly three years since Robert completed my guitar. Except for the times I've been away, I've played it every day, getting to know it better and keeping that Sitka spruce top vibrating so that the guitar will have the chance to open up and reach its full potential in my lifetime. After wondering if I would see it finished, I now wonder how long I'll be around to play it and what will come of it when I'm gone.

I recently turned sixty-six. Even if I live a normal lifespan – and that's far from certain – I probably have at best fourteen years of playing time left. If I depart this earth when I'm eighty, my guitar will be seventeen years old, a mere teenager. It could easily have a life journey of its own of a hundred years or more if taken care of. Robert's construction method using hide glue and French polish that make for easy repair has insured that in the right hands it could exist far into the future, outliving even my own children and grandchildren. It's odd to think of that, to think of a human artifact outliving a human being, but of course they do.

As for Robert, he's moved on to new undertakings. Our archtop project marked a significant turning point for him. He's now building violins. This from his partner Susan:

"The process of prototyping your archtop initiated a major shift in Robert's life as a luthier. I'm thinking here about his trip to England. Receiving the validation of an arts grant was empowering, yes. But for Robert it was more about something else. He still lights up when he talks about spending two weeks in Juliet's school [Juliet Barker, founder of the Cambridge Violin Makers Workshop], watching an eighty-something-year-old demonstrate a lifetime of skill, and learning from her to discern the precise placement of f-holes, and how to know when to stop carving! But the real shift is how it has opened up for Robert the world of building the violin family of instruments, and I think that may be where his heart takes him for years to come. Thank you for that, Rick!"

That paragraph (part of a longer note Susan wrote in response to reading a draft of this book), pleases me. It's nice to know that my archtop has spawned new projects for Robert and opened new horizons. In fact he recently built a violin that was featured in the *One Tree* exhibit at the Robert Bateman Gallery here in Victoria. He was one of a select group of artisans invited to craft an artifact from a giant Big Leaf maple tree that was felled in the Cowichan valley. Quite an honour and quite a violin – I saw it recently and was enthralled by its graceful beauty.

He continues to build guitars – in fact he recently completed a new flat-top design for Eric Schoenberg – but violin building is giving him a lot of pleasure, perhaps as much as I'm deriving from my guitar, which is considerable.

And what of perfection? Did we achieve it? Did Robert build me a perfect guitar?

There's no question he built me a great guitar. A professional artist friend of mine who is a sculptor and guitar player was very taken with it and spontaneously called it a "work of art" when he held it and played it some months ago. That unsolicited compliment from a discerning artist affirmed its aesthetic qualities. Visually it's a beautiful instrument and sonically it has a richness I still haven't heard in other archtops I've played.

The real test, of course, is that I love to play it. It's hard to walk by it without picking it up and sitting down for a time to enjoy its look, feel and sound. I sometimes move to another instrument but I always come back to hear the richness of tone and appreciate the elegance of design Robert achieved. As I say, I play it almost every day.

Occasionally I still find myself re-imagining what we built. How would it sound if we'd used a metal tailpiece connector? How would a thumbwheel-equipped bridge that could raise or lower the action change the experience of playing it? How would it sound amplified? And in my most extreme moments – what if I got Robert to remove the top and change the bracing from parallel braces to a X-braces, a style more common on modern archtop guitars. What difference would that make?

I acted on one of these impulses over a year ago and purchased a Benedetto floating humbucker pickup designed specifically for an acoustic archtop. It's now installed on the ebony pickguard Robert made and sounds incredible through my jazz amp. As jazz players everywhere have found, there's a kind of sonic perfection in the marriage of an acoustic archtop with a magnetic pickup. A little electronic boost adds the needed body to create that warm jazz sound that is like nothing else on this planet. The truth is though, I mostly play the guitar acoustically, the way it was designed.

I continue to look at other guitars. A year after I brought the archtop home, inspired by Bill Frisell's and Ted Greene's solo work on their vintage telecasters, I had a fling with solid body electrics and purchased a beautiful G&L ASAT Classic telecaster-style electric guitar. Sometimes it's the only guitar I want to play. But then my ears grow tired of the purely electric sound and I'll come downstairs to the living room (my electric guitars live upstairs in my music room) and gratefully pick up the archtop again and hear with fresh ears its rich acoustic sound.

Six months after buying the G & L, I bought an East-man acoustic parlour guitar modelled after the early small-bodied instruments that graced North American homes in the late nineteenth century. Comfortable to hold, with a warm sound well-suited to fingerstyle playing, parlour guitars have made a comeback. With the neck joining the body at the twelfth fret, it's the easiest of all my instruments to play and produces amazing volume and decent tone with little effort. But as full and loud as the sound is, it just doesn't compare with the rich tonal palette of the archtop.

I continue to imagine new instruments. If I had the funds, I'd probably work with Robert on designing and building a smaller, thinner-bodied cutaway archtop constructed specifically with amplification in mind. Something more contemporary than the instrument we produced but not so out there that it loses its connection with tradition. I imagine a guitar somewhere between traditional and contemporary, maybe with a laminate top and back to discourage feedback, a single humbucker mounted on the body near the neck and a fretboard well-suited to fingerstyle playing. Or maybe it would be a chambered solid-body with f-holes, or maybe ... I could go on.

I've come to accept that I'll always suffer from the restlessness of the seeker. That's my nature but it's also the nature of the guitar, the most malleable of all instruments. With its aesthetic and auditory shape-shifting, the guitar can take on infinite forms and sounds. All the possibilities cannot possibly be contained in one instrument.

I realize now that for the guitar player there can be no Shangri-La, no pot of gold, no finality. As with learning to play an instrument, as with living life itself, perfection is found only in the seeking.

ACKNOWLEDGEMENTS

My wife Pat has always been my number one sup-
porter and I want to thank her for her forbearance
and gentle spirit. She was an early reader of the manuscript
and contributed a number of helpful suggestions.

My son Matt, who has pursued music by composing,
performing and producing and by building a successful
recording studio, has long inspired me with his vision,
independent spirit, and persistence.

My daughter Claire has always shared my love for
ideas and language. Her interest in my writing and in
this project inspired me to keep going and see it through.

My adopted brothers in music and life, Ron and
Dennis Bull, have been with me literally from birth.
Their enthusiastic support for this project and our days
of playing and being together have meant the world to
me.

My friend and comrade-in-arms from university
days, Allan Wilson, was an early reader of the
manuscript and made many helpful suggestions. Allan
inspires me every day by embracing life despite losing
his only child to cancer.

My friend, the novelist D.F. Bailey, first suggested
that we swap editorial duties while he worked on a

new novel and I worked on this book. His support and suggestions have guided and encouraged me every step of the way.

I'm deeply grateful to Linda Manzer for her generous, warm spirit and willingness to run with my idea for a radio documentary even though she didn't know me from a hole in the ground.

Pat Metheny also supported the documentary and welcomed me to his home studio in NYC. My interviews with Pat and Linda remain the highlight of my journalistic career and have everything to do with the creation of this book.

Julian Lage, Frank Vignola, and Bucky Pizzarelli are three of the world's greatest jazz guitar players. Their willingness to pick up the phone and chat with me about archtop guitars was a dream come true.

Robert Anderson's partner Susan Ellenton has shared friendship, music, and ideas with me and was an early reader of the manuscript. Her honest reactions and warm support made the book better.

Finally, this book and my archtop guitar wouldn't exist without Robert Anderson. I want to thank Robert for his friendship, his incredible skill as an instrument maker and his willingness to go along with my crazy idea. I'll never forget that year in his workshop.

My sincere apologies to anyone I've inadvertently forgotten to mention.

BIBLIOGRAPHY

"About Schoenberg Guitars." Schoenberg Guitars Schoenberg Guitars, n.d. Web. 20 April 2012.

Anderson, Robert. Personal Interview. August 2009.

Anderson, Robert. Personal Interview. 22 May 2013

Benedetto, Robert. *Making An Archtop Guitar.* Anaheim Hills, CA: Centerstream Publishing, 1994.

Beimborn, Dan and Meador, Rob. "A Brief History of the Mandolin." Mandolin Cafe. Mandolin Cafe, n.d. Web. n.d.

Bramwell, Martyn. *The International Book of Wood.* London: Mitchell Beazley Publishers Ltd., 1976.

Cerra, Steven A. "The Four Freshman: A Vocal Quartet with Quarter Tones." Jazz Profiles. Jazz Profiles, 22 November 2011. Web. n.d.

Crowe, Julia. *My First Guitar: Tales of True Love and Lost Chords From 70 Legendary Musicians.* Toronto: ECW Press, 2012.

Dudley, Kathryn Marie. *Guitar Makers: The Endurance of Artisanal Values in North America.* Chicago and London: University of Chicago Press, 2014.

Evans, Stephen. "The Sweet Sound of Success." BBC News. BBC, 17 March 2013. Web. n.d.

Faber, Tony. *Stradivarius: Five Violins, One Cello, and a Genius.* London: Macmillan, 2004.

Freeland, Cynthia. *But Is It Art: An Introduction to*

Art Theory. Oxford: Oxford University Press, 2001.

Gibbs, Rick. "For the Love of the Guitar." *Boulevard Magazine*, November 2009.

Green, Harvey. *Wood: Craft, Culture, History.* New York: Viking Penguin, 2006.

"Guitar Heroes: Legendary Craftsmen from Italy to New York." Metropolitan Museum of Art, 9 February - 4 July, 2011. Metropolitan Museum.Web. n.d.

Guy, Paul. "A Brief History of the Guitar." Guitar Handbook. Paul Guy, 2001-2007. Web. n.d.

Hannan, Michael T. "History of the Organization of Work." *Encyclopaedia Britannica*, n.d. Web. n.d.

Ham, James. "New Projects." James Ham Luthier. James Ham, n.d. Web. 12 February 2012.

Helmholtz, Hermann I.F. *On the Sensations of Tone As a Physiological Basis for the Theory of Music.* London: Longmann, Green and Co., 1885, Kindle ebook.

Hernandez, Gabriel. "Benedetto Talks Archtops in Nashville." *Premier Guitar.* Premier Guitar, 2 September 2009. Web. n.d.

Herrod, Chris. "Alternative Tonewoods." Luthiers Mercantile International. LMI: 20 May 2004. Web. 30 January 2012.

Jaen, Fernando Alonso. "The Archtop Jazz Guitar." *Acoustic Fingerstyle Guitar.* Acoustic Fingerstyle Guitar: n.d. Web. 27 February 2013.

Kaye, Lenny. "The Vibrating String." Dangerous Curves: The Art of the Guitar. Museum of Musical Instruments. April 2000. Web. 8 March 2012.

Kidder, Tracy. *House.* New York: Mariner Books,1999.

Lage, Julian. Phone Interview. 13 July 2014.

Laird, Ross A. *Grain of Truth: The Ancient Lessons*

of Craft. Toronto, Ontario: Macfarlane, Walter and Ross, 2001

Levitin, Daniel. *This is Your Brain on Music*. Toronto: Plume, Penguin Group, 2007.

"Markneukirchen." Wikipedia. Wikimedia Foundation, n.d. Web. n.d.

"The Martin Story." About Martin. C.F. Martin Co., n.d. Web. n.d.

Manzer, Linda. Personal Interview. 14 November 2010

Metheny, Pat. Personal Interview. 16 November 2010

Miller, Bryan. "Saving Gibson Guitars from the Musical Scrap Heap." *New York Times*. 13 March 1994. Web. 31 January 2012.

Monteleone, John. Email Interview. 20 January 2016.

"Nitrocellulose." Wikipedia. Wikimedia Foundation, n.d. Web. n.d.

"Picea Sitchensis." *The Gymnosperm Database*. 22 May 2011. Web. 20 February 2012.

Pickrell, John. "Did the 'Little Ice Age' Create Stradivarius Violins' Famous Tone?" *National Geographic News*. National Geographic. 7 January 2004. Web. 20 February 2012.

Pizzarelli, Bucky. Phone Interview. 24 July 2014

Pojar, Jim and MacKinnon, Andy. *Plants of the Pacific Northwest*. BC: BC Ministry of Forests and Lone Pine Publishing, 1994

"Progressions: 100 Years of Jazz Guitar." CD Collection Booklet. Sony BMG, 2005.

Ronstadt, Linda. *Simple Dreams: A Musical Memoir*. New York: Simon and Schuster, 2013.

Rybczynski, Witold. *The Most Beautiful House in the World*. New York: Viking Penguin, 1989

Rzepczynski, Kris. "Gibson Inc., Music Makers."

Kalamazoo Public Library, 1998. Web. 8 March 2012.

Schmid, Paul William. *Acquired of the Angels: The Lives and Works of Master Guitar Makers John D'Angelico and James L. D'Aquisto.* Metuchen, NJ: Scarecrow Press, 1991.

Siminoff, Roger. "Orville H. Gibson 1856-1918." Siminoff Banjo and Mandolin. 2010. Web. 8 March 2012.

Siminoff, Roger. "Lloyd Loar: The Man Inside the Name." Siminoff Banjo and Mandolin. 2013. Web. 12 February 2014.

Siminoff, Roger. "Lloyd Allayre Loar." Siminoff Banjo and Mandolin. 2010. Web. 8 March 2012.

Somogyi, Ervin. "Some Thoughts on the Difference Between Handmade and Factory Made Guitars." Ervin Somogyi, 2010. Web. n.d.

"The Steinway Soundboard." Steinway Pianos. n.d. Web. 20 February 2012.

Vignola, Frank. Phone Interview. 22 July 2014

Vose, Ken. *Blue Guitar.* San Francisco, CA: Chronicle Books, 1998.

Wade, Graham. *A Concise History of the Classic Guitar.* Pacific, MO: Mel Bay, 2001.

Wahl-Stephens, Gavin. "Nitro vs. Poly." Pro Guitar Shop, 16 December 2011. Web. n.d.

Wegst, Ulrike G. K. "Wood for Sound" *American Journal of Botany,* 93.10 (2006): 1439-1448. Web.

Wolfe, Joe. "Violin Acoustics: An Introduction." University of New South Wales. UNSW, n.d. Web. 8 March 2012.

PERMISSIONS

I'm grateful to the following individuals and companies for the generous permissions they've provided.

Centerstream Publishing for quotations used from *Making an Archtop Guitar* by Robert Benedetto.

John Monteleone for quotations from the Met blog "Guitar Heroes: Legendary Craftsmen from Italy to New York."

Ken Vose for quotations used from his book *Blue Guitar*.

Linda Manzer and Pat Metheny for quotations used from interviews conducted for *Kindred Spirits: Linda Manzer's Thirty Year Journey with Pat Metheny*

Ross A. Laird for quotations used from his book *Grain of Truth: The Ancient Lessons of Craft*.

Scarecrow Press (Rowman and Littlefield) for quotations used from *Acquired of the Angels* by Paul William Schmid.

TEN GREAT ARCHTOP RECORDINGS

Moonglow Frank Vignola and Bucky Pizzarelli
Sounding Point Julian Lage*
Double Standard Martin Taylor
Smokin' at the Half Note Wes Montgomery
Live Jim Hall
Virtuoso Joe Pass
Genius of the Electric Guitar Charlie Christian
Legends: Solo Guitar Performances George Van Eps
and Johnny Smith
Midnight Blue Kenny Burrell
Beyond the Missouri Sky Pat Metheny and Charlie
Haden**

*Lage plays a Martin D-18GE acoustic flat-top on this
album in addition to his Linda-Manzer-built archtop.

**This is not an archtop album per se. I include it
because it's a wonderful album for hearing the beauty
of Metheny's (and Haden's) playing and of Linda
Manzer's incredible guitars from her nylon string
to her sitar guitar to the amazing forty-two string
"Pikasso."

Visit the following websites.

robertandersonguitars.com

www.rickgibbs.ca

www.cadencehousepress.com

www.islandjazz.ca

ABOUT THE AUTHOR

Music articles written by Rick Gibbs have appeared in *Monday Magazine, Coda, Boulevard Magazine* and *Penguin Eggs*. He wrote, produced, and presented *Kindred Spirits: Linda Manzer's Thirty-Year Journey with Pat Metheny,* a one-hour CBC radio documentary about the musical relationship between guitarist Pat Metheny and Canadian guitar builder Linda Manzer. He lives with his wife in Victoria, BC, where when he's not writing, he studies jazz guitar.